A Forest of Quilts

Designs for Those Who Love the Outdoors

Terrie Kralik

©2003 Terrie Kralik

Published by

kp krause publications
An F&W Publications Company

700 East State Street • Iola, WI 54990-0001
715-445-2214 • 888-457-2873
www.krause.com

Please call or write for our free catalog of publications. Our toll-free number to place an order or obtain a free catalog is 800-258-0929, or please use our regular business telephone 715-445-2214.

Photos on the following pages were taken
by Terrie Kralik: 3, 4, 5, 6, 7, 98, 128.

Library of Congress Catalog Number: 2002113146

ISBN: 0-87349-553-5

Acknowledgments

Thank you to many of my quilting friends who have contributed their ideas and designs for this book. I appreciate your enthusiasm and thank you for being part of this exciting endeavor. A special thank you to my family, who has gently encouraged me to pursue my dreams of all things quilted. It couldn't have happened without you!

Table of Contents

Introduction

What do you have in your forest? I find all kinds of wild animals—some apprehensive, some curious, some who leave only tracks, some that chatter at you as you walk by. Then there are the trees and plants that hide the animals and bugs, flowers that feed them, leaves, and needles as the seasons change. What I find most rewarding is the peace you feel as you share this wonderful part of our country with its native animals. The stress of the day just slips away, and you experience a peace of mind that can't be found anywhere else.

I have tried to capture some of those peaceful moments for you in fabric. I've compiled several different animal designs, mixed and matched them with a variety of borders and filler units that quilters love to sew, and put together oodles of projects. I'm hoping you will want to make one of these projects first, and then become inspired to branch out and try designing your very own project.

Admittedly, most quilters begin by copying the work that someone else has done, often trying to duplicate it color-for-color, fabric-for-fabric. The more experienced you become, the more you have the urge to do something different, to step out of your comfort zone and try something new. To help you move in that direction, I have included a section that explains how to make your project uniquely your own, plus photos of some great examples.

Be sure to read my suggestions for fabric selection. Notice that most projects are shown in different color combinations, so enjoy looking at each for *color ideas* in addition to *arrangement ideas*.

The wallhanging projects in Chapter 3 are arranged with some intended order, even though they don't appear to be. The first few projects include only one animal or subject in several different poses, in different sizes, and fitted onto different-sized background pieces. The drawings of the animals and plants can be found at the back of the book. They have already been reversed so they are ready to trace with fusible web.

Towards the end of the chapter, you will find projects that combine different elements already shown—maybe taking an elk from one project, a tree from another, and a paw print from yet a different project. Nearly all the center designs of these wallhangings are based on a 12" finished square and are completely interchangeable. The majority of the other elements are also interchangeable. Here's where your own creativity comes in. After seeing all these combinations, you're bound to want to make your own design. Let yourself go!

Did you notice that most of the borders and filler designs are different? That continues throughout the majority of wallhanging designs. And again, make your own borders if you'd like. If you love checkerboards, find a wallhanging design that is close to the arrangement you like, and tweak it here and there as needed. Maybe the paw print you want to add is too small. Would two or three of them look better in that larger space? Maybe fill the extra space with some more checkerboards. Just try it!

After the wallhangings come other projects—a simple quilt in several sizes designed to take advantage of the wonderful animal and novelty prints available, a row quilt with lots of fun patterns, a tablecloth and table runner, pillows, plus ideas on using the designs for clothing.

Specific directions for piecing the filler parts like checkerboards, flying geese, and half-square triangles, are explained in the Techniques section. As a quilt teacher, I understand that diagrams are an essential part of directions, and I have included *lots* of them. Beginners will love this section and will be able to add some more useful piecing tricks to their sewing basket, whether they are taking a class or learning on their own.

Quilt teachers, check out the section just for you—For Teachers Only. I've included a newsletter description and suggested class outlines for four different classes, each with a different focus and geared towards different skill levels. The complete section on piecing techniques has so much information packed into it that most of your class prep work has been done for you! And with most samples being done with different color combinations, you'll be able to help your students be successful with their choices.

Most importantly, enjoy yourself as you make these projects. Put your creativity to work for you as you choose the perfect fabrics for one of my projects, or design your own project using the elements I've given. Sit back and enjoy the satisfaction of completing a project of nature!

CHAPTER 1
The Basics

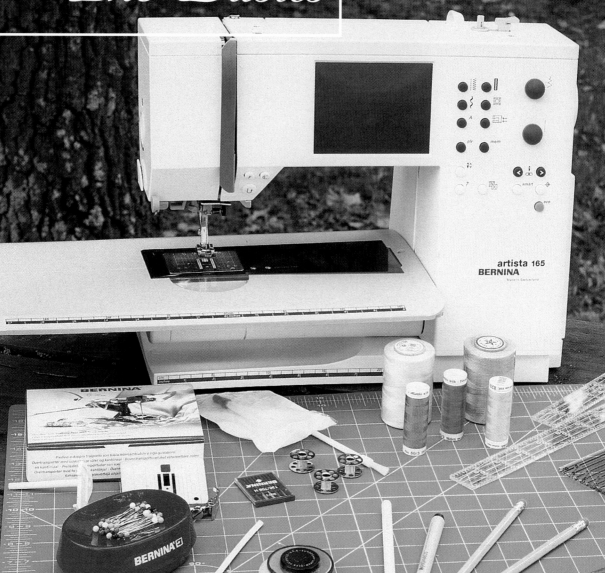

General Instructions

Terminology

Conversations are so much better when we speak the same language, so I've compiled a short list to explain some quilter talk I use in the book. You may already be familiar with many of these words or phrases, but just in case, I've given my interpretation of them. Quilters are always coming up with new terms!

Audition fabric—To literally lay out the fabrics you wish to use in a project with others that will be in it, to see if the fabrics are as effective as you want. Auditioning is often done to determine the best fabrics and widths to make borders.

Chunk—A portion cut from a strata, or a portion of pieced units sewn together into a bigger unit. Same as segment.

Cross-cut—To cut across seams, usually across seams of a strata unit, often forming a portion of a block or border.

Design wall—A design surface covered with punch fleece or flannel that allows placement of blocks or pieces without pinning. It allows you not only to see how something will look after it is sewn, but it also allows you to move things around and try other arrangements.

Easing—Evenly working in the excess fabric as you sew, matching the length of a longer unit with a shorter one. This is often done with borders or when sewing two blocks of similar but unequal size.

Finished size—The size of a block or unit after all seams have been sewn.

RSO—Right sides out.

RST—Right sides together.

RSU—Right side up.

Segment—A portion cut from a strata.

Strata—Two or more strips of fabric of varying widths and length sewn together to form a larger piece of fabric.

Strip—A strip of fabric cut on the cross-grain, cut from selvage to selvage, making a piece that is the width specified and approximately 45" long.

Unfinished size—The size of a block or unit before sewing all outer seams; projects will often give the unfinished measurements of units or blocks so you can square up that portion before moving on.

WST—Wrong sides together.

WSU—Wrong side up.

Sewing machine and rulers courtesy of The Sampler House, Stevens Point, Wis.

Tools Needed

Here are the basic tools you will need to make the projects in this book:

- Sewing machine—Make sure it really works!! Have it serviced regularly, and change the needle often.

- Basic sewing kit—100% cotton thread, pins, seam ripper, marking tools, etc.

- Basic rotary cutting equipment—a rotary cutter and mat

- Rulers—6" x 12", 6" x 24", and ruler at least 12½" square

- Marking tools—#2 pencil, chalk pencil
  Other helpful tools include:

- 6" Bias Square ruler by That Patchwork Place

- 6" Add-a-Quarter ruler by CM Designs

- That Purple Thang by Little Foot Ltd., a stylus, or a bamboo chopstick

- Walking foot for sewing machine

- ¼" foot for sewing machine

- Straight stitch throat plate

- Black permanent marking pen, like a Micron .05

- Tweezers

Piecing Tips

- If you have two different throat plates for your sewing machine, use the one designed for a straight stitch.

- Set your sewing machine needle to stop in the down position.

- Chain sew as much as possible. This means to sew one seam right after another, without cutting the threads between pieces. Do this for speed and accuracy. If you are repeatedly sewing the same pieces together, you will notice a misplaced piece more often if chain sewing.

- Square up and trim to size your half-square triangle units with the Bias Square, aligning the diagonal line on the ruler with the seam.

- Take care of your sewing machine by cleaning the lint out of it and oiling it regularly.

- Replace machine needles regularly. A bent or damaged needle can make a big difference in your stitch quality.

- Use That Purple Thang or your stylus to help guide your fabric through the sewing machine. It's especially helpful when sewing over bulky seams and intersections.

Using Fusible Web

Due to the nature of fusible webs, what you see and what you get are not the same. The designs found in the back of the book have been reversed so they will face the correct direction when fused onto your background fabric for each project.

Tip: If you are creating your own wallhanging and wish the design to face the other direction, copy the given design on tracing paper. Turn your paper over, and trace the design on the reverse side. Use this new design when you trace it onto fusible web.

In general, follow these steps when using fusible web:

1. Trace appliqué shapes individually onto the paper side of your fusible web. Allow about ½" between pieces. Dashed lines show where pieces will overlap. The dashed area is under another piece.

2. Loosely cut out each piece, about ¼" larger than drawn. Follow the fusible web manufacturer's instructions to iron them to the wrong side of your selected fabrics.

3. Cut out each piece directly on the drawn lines. Remove the paper from each piece.

4. Position pieces as indicated in the photos or as you prefer. Iron in place as directed by manufacturer, following time and temperature guidelines.

5. Finish the raw edges of your design as desired. This is an optional step, but it makes the designs more durable and less likely to fray. The most common way to finish the edges is with machine appliqué, a very tight zigzag stitch sewn on your machine.

Fusible Web Tips

- Heat is critical! Test to determine the best iron temperature to use with your web. Each brand is different, and some will be ruined by too much heat or not fused well with the heat set too low or ironed too short a time. Follow the manufacturer's directions.

- Remove the paper backing from your pieces carefully. The smaller or skinnier the piece (like flower stems, antlers, and legs), the easier it is for the fabric itself to tear as you remove the paper. Be gentle!

- If the webbing separates as you try to pull off the paper backing, the piece wasn't ironed long enough. Re-iron.

- OOPS? Just cut off a leg or antler, or cut a tree wrong? Sometimes the pieces can be overlapped slightly and fused down. Sometimes the cut off area can be omitted. Does the piece look okay without it? Then there are times where you have to cut out another piece and start over. You have to make a decision on this one.

- Tweezers help to pick up and place small pieces. A long pin with a large head works equally well.

- Use sharp, pointed, small fabric scissors to cut out your fused pieces. Dull blades will tear the fabric and leave an unattractive frayed edge.

- When cutting, hold your scissors stationary and move the fabric around the scissors as you cut out your design. You will have better control this way.

- If you have fused several designs to a large piece of fabric, cut them apart so you can accurately cut out each individual design without the bulk of the extra fabric.

- To make your animals appear even more lifelike, cut the "fur" areas (like the bear or elk's neck) with a wiggling motion so the finished look is uneven.

- Cutting the tiny points like the bear claws and eagle talons can be tricky. The easiest way is to cut up to the claw, around all of them in a clump, and then go back and clip out the area between the claws. Some of the antlers can be done this way also.

- Use a ruler to align the animals on the background piece. Usually line up the animals based on the lower raw edge of the background.

- Generally center your pieces on the background fabric and allow for a ¼" seam allowance.

- Take your time when you're cutting many pieces. It can be very fatiguing to your cutting hand and your eyes, so take a break now and then. Don't cut them all in one sitting, especially if you already have damage to your wrist.

- Most designs can be fused to their background area after the top is pieced. This keeps your designs fresh and sharp looking. Note: Any design that extends into the seam allowance should be fused in place before that seam is sewn, such as the edge of some trees and branches, the "horizon line" behind the scene of the moose, etc.

- Store your fusible web rolled up in a large roll rather than tightly wound up. This way the glued surface will not release from the paper side as easily during storage.

- I have discovered that most fusible webs seem to have a shelf life. If you are having problems with your particular product not adhering as you think it should, get a new piece and see if that one works any better. If not, try another product, perhaps one that sticks to your fabric and is fused in place at the end.

Techniques

Half-Square Triangles

This is one of my favorite ways to make half-square triangles. If you have a different way that works for you, use it!! The end result will be the same. With this technique, you yield two units for every pair of fabrics.

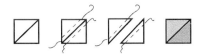

Tip: If you have tried this method before and you always end up with a unit that is too small, add ⅛" to your initial cutting measurements and follow the rest of the steps. For example, if your pattern says to cut 3⅞" squares for half-square triangles, cut them 4" square. This should give you a little extra to work with when you trim the units to size.

1. Cut an equal number of light and dark squares of the same size (finished size of square + ⅞").

2. Mark a diagonal line on the wrong side of each light fabric.

3. Place one light and one dark RST.

4. Stitch ¼" away from the drawn line, on both sides of the line.

5. Cut on the drawn line.

6. Press seams to the dark side.

7. Square up to the correct size, trimming off points. (I prefer to use the Bias Square ruler for this step, aligning the 45-degree angle on the seam line.)

Speedy Triangles

This is a fun technique that can be used in a lot of places where you need to add a triangle to a rectangle or square. It has several other names, such as fast-corner triangles, quick triangles, connector squares, etc. It is quick and simple and pretty accurate, but does have some waste.

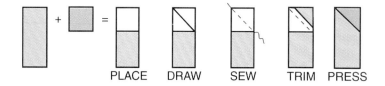

PLACE   DRAW   SEW   TRIM   PRESS

1. In general, place the triangle fabric (currently a square) RST in the corner of the square or rectangle it is added to.

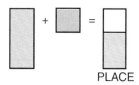

PLACE

2. On the wrong side of the triangle fabric, draw a diagonal line from corner to corner,

DRAW

3. and sew on this line.

SEW

4. Trim off the outside corner of the triangle fabric only. As a general rule of thumb, do not trim the original square or rectangle.

TRIM

5.Press to the corner.

PRESS

Square-in-a-Square

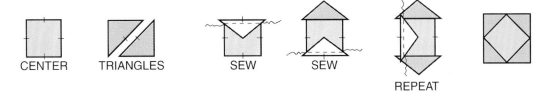

CENTER   TRIANGLES   SEW   SEW   REPEAT

1. Cut the center square the size specified. This piece can be fussy-cut or specifically cut to center a chosen motif, regardless of the grainline of the fabric. Keep in mind that ¼" around all sides will become the seam allowance.

2. Outer corner triangles begin as squares, cut once on the diagonal.

CENTER   TRIANGLES

3. Mark the center point of all sides of the center square and the long side of each triangle.

4. Place a triangle RST on opposite sides of the center square, aligning center points. Sew each with a ¼" seam. Press to the triangle. Repeat for the remaining two opposite sides.

SEW   SEW   REPEAT

Tip: You are sewing bias edges. Sew slowly and pin as needed to minimize distortion. Press gently!

5. Square up the blocks to the correct size. Make sure you leave ¼" seam allowance as measured from the points of your block.

Fast Flying Geese

This is my favorite way to make flying geese, and it's useful when sewing multiples of the same fabric combination. In this method, one large square plus four small squares yields four flying geese units of identical color. You may have leftover units. For example, if your project requires 15 flying geese, you will make 16 with this method. One is excess.

> **Tip:** To make somewhat scrappy flying geese, use a variety of fabrics of the same color value for the small square, and a combination of similar value fabrics for the large square. Each large square will make four units of that color, but the various small squares will help make it look scrappier.

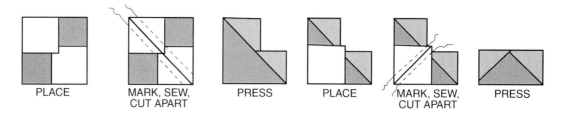

PLACE   MARK, SEW, CUT APART   PRESS   PLACE   MARK, SEW, CUT APART   PRESS

1. Begin by cutting the size and number of pieces listed for your particular project. Remember, there will be a ratio of four small squares to one large square. Draw a diagonal line on the wrong side of every small square, using whatever tool works for that fabric (sharp No. 2 pencil, white chalk pencil, or colored pencil).

2. Lay one large square right side up in front of you. Place one small square RST in one corner and diagonally opposite, aligning edges and drawn lines. Their points will overlap in the middle.

PLACE

3. Sew ¼" away from the drawn line, on both sides of the line. Cut on the drawn line.

MARK, SEW, CUT APART

4. Press toward the smaller pieces.

PRESS

5. Lay a small square RST in the remaining 90° corner of the dark print. The point and drawn line of the small square should extend between the two sewn triangles.

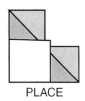

PLACE

6. Sew ¼" away from the drawn line, on both sides of it. Cut on the drawn line. Press toward the smaller piece. Repeat. Trim points.

MARK, SEW, CUT APART

7. Trim to the correct size (listed in your project directions).

There are other ways to make flying geese. One of those is to use the Speedy Triangle method, where you begin with a rectangle of fabric that will be the large triangle area of the flying geese. To this are added squares sewn diagonally on each side. If this method is used, you will be referred to the Speedy Triangle technique for complete instructions. I would choose this method if I really wanted a scrappy effect and didn't have many flying geese to make. Note that there is some waste with this method.

Checkerboard

Most checkerboards in this book are pieced with a speed technique using strips of fabric rather than using small squares.

1. Sew strips of light and dark fabrics together along their longest side using an accurate ¼"

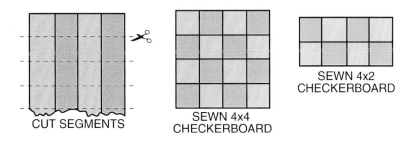

CUT SEGMENTS

SEWN 4x4 CHECKERBOARD

SEWN 4x2 CHECKERBOARD

seam. The actual sizes of the strips will be given in each project and allow for some excess but not a lot.

2. Press toward the dark fabric.

3. For accuracy, verify that this strata is the correct width as listed in your project, and adjust stitching if necessary.

4. Cut across these strips to make smaller segments. The actual size to cross-cut will be given in your project, but it is usually the same measurement as the width of the initial strips.

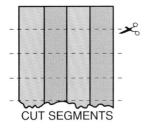

CUT SEGMENTS

5. Sew segments together, alternating placement of color to form your checkerboard. Your project will tell you how many segments form the finished unit size, and it will give a finished size to compare your actual size to.

6. Press seams all in one direction, or press them open.

Tip: For large checkerboard units, you may be sewing many strips together into a large strata before cross-cutting them into segments. Smaller checkerboards may be sewn with only two. The process is the same regardless.

Strip-Pieced Border

Strip piecing is used to create a scrappy border using many fabrics or to create a filler section made of strips. The technique is the same, and you can choose from several variations.

In general, follow these instructions to make a Strip-Pieced border:

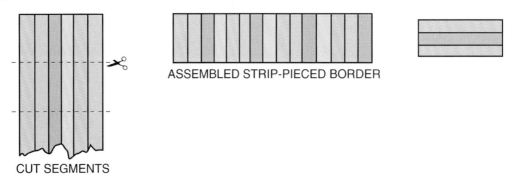

CUT SEGMENTS

ASSEMBLED STRIP-PIECED BORDER

1. Cut strips of varying widths and lengths, or as suggested in your specific project, and sew the strips together using a ¼" seam. Press all seams in one direction. This unit is now called a strata. Verify that the width of your strata is the same as given in your project. Make adjustments if necessary by taking wider or narrower seams and pressing well.

2. Cut segments of this strata to the width specified or to your liking. Sew enough segments together to make the length you need for the border or filler unit, trimming to the exact length. Sew the border to the quilt top, following the directions for borders. See Chapter 2, Finishing Your Project.

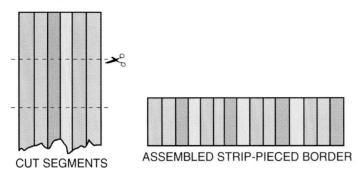

CUT SEGMENTS   ASSEMBLED STRIP-PIECED BORDER

Variations:
- Use all the same width strips and a consistent repeated pattern of fabrics (e.g. red, white, blue, red, white, blue).
- For a scrappy look, each strip could be a different fabric.
- You may want to make two or three different strata, each with a different combination and order of fabrics.
- Vary the width of the fabrics for added interest, and keep the accent fabrics narrower than the other fabrics so they *accent,* not overpower.
- Position strata segments around your project asymmetrically, in a pleasing manner. I prefer to lay this out on my design wall and see how it looks before I commit to sewing the segments together, or before sewing the strips to the project.

Mountains (Half an Hourglass)

Instructions here are for a variation of an hourglass, appearing to be dimensional mountains. The units are sewn like a half-square triangle, plus a few more steps. Begin with the larger squares, your light and medium fabrics.

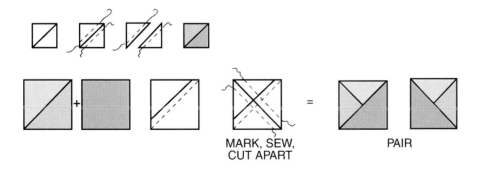

MARK, SEW,   PAIR
CUT APART

1. Cut squares of fabric as directed.

2. Mark a diagonal line on the wrong side of each light fabric.

3. Place one light and one medium square RST.

4. Stitch ¼" away from the drawn line, on both sides of the line.

5. Cut on the drawn line.

6. Press seams to the medium side.

7. Square up to the correct size, trimming off points. (I prefer to use the Bias Square ruler to align the 45-degree angle on the seam line.) You have just completed a half-square triangle. Repeat as needed.

8. Mark a diagonal line on the wrong side of each half-square triangle unit, across the seam (crossing the seam rather than aligned with it).

9. Place a dark square RST with a half-square triangle Stitch ¼" away from the drawn line, on both sides of the line. Cut on the drawn line. Press to the large dark triangle.

10. Square up to the correct size, trimming off points. (Remember to use the Bias Square ruler to make this job easier.)

Note: This process makes a mirror image pair of "mountain" units.

Tall Pines

These pieces can be made with or without an added trunk, and they could be used as arrow points instead of trees, depending on their placement and coloration. This is a variation of the Speedy Triangle technique.

1. Cut the pieces as listed in the project.

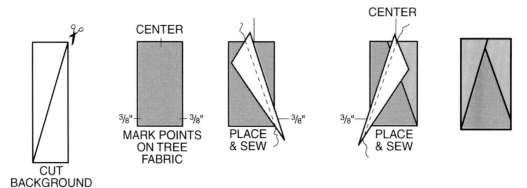

2. Place two background pieces RST. Cut once on the diagonal. This yields four pieces and makes the mirror image pieces you will need, which is enough background pieces for two trees. Pair up the mirror images to make the rest of the process easier—one will face right, one left.

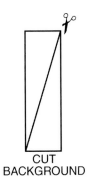

CUT
BACKGROUND

3. Place each tree piece RSU in front of you, aligned as it will be in the finished tree. (If your tree is 4½" wide and 4 ¾" tall, lay it out so the width is 4½". Yes, this is important! Other rectangular shapes will be easier to lay out properly.)

4. Mark the center point at the top raw edge. Mark a point ⅜" up from the lower edge on each side.

CENTER

3/8" 3/8"

MARK POINTS
ON TREE
FABRIC

5. Place backgrounds on top of trees, as if they were already sewn. Remove one, and flip the other as you position it to sew, placing the background triangle RST with the tree triangle. Align the background with marks on the tree fabric so the long raw edge lines up with the top center point and side point. A point of the background piece will extend ¼" above the upper edge of the tree fabric, and well beyond the lower edge.

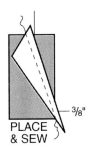

3/8"

PLACE
& SEW

6. Pin or hold in place and gently flip over as if sewn. If the background completely covers the tree fabric in that corner area, you've positioned the background correctly and it's ready to sew. If it's not aligned correctly, reposition, pin, and check again until it's right. Stitch ¼" from the raw edge of the long side of the triangle piece.

7. Press to the background. Trim seam to ¼" using an Add-a-Quarter ruler and removing any excess tree fabric.

8. Mark the center point at the top raw edge again (based on your tree fabric). Repeat Steps 5, 6, and 7.

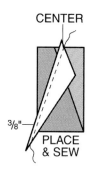

CENTER

3/8"

PLACE & SEW

9. Square up the unit to the correct measurement, allowing at least a ¼" seam allowance above the top point of tree.

10. Add trunks, if desired, using the Strip-Pieced Border technique.

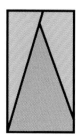

CHAPTER 2
Put It Together

Beginning Your Project

Fabric Selection

Sometimes the hardest part of a project is getting started. Do you begin with a pattern you like and then choose fabrics, or do you choose fabrics first and then decide what to do with them? This is definitely a personal choice. Both methods work equally well, and I'm sure you've tried them both, just like I have.

To give you an idea of how I generally go about choosing and placing fabrics, I'll walk you through my thought process, and you can help me make those decisions. For this exercise, I have chosen the wallhanging project that I want to make, and I'm now ready to select fabrics.

I begin by looking at multi-print fabrics, watching for one that calls out to me or a combination of colors that jumps into my arms. What strikes me on a warm sunny afternoon is definitely different than what appeals to me as crisp autumn leaves begin to fall. This selection can be done at home, looking through your personal stash, or at your local quilt shop. Just make sure when the fabric talks to you, you don't talk back!

Now that I've selected the main fabric, I will use the colors within it to add to my choices and accent my favorites. Look at the selvage edge of the main fabric, and you will probably find a chart of colored circles. These are the colors that were used to print the fabric. Take advantage of the work already done, and match fabrics to these colors! Start with darks and mediums, varying the print of additional fabrics. Include different textures, geometrics, florals, stripes, curves, tone-on-tones, etc. The more variety you have, the better. I haven't decided yet where I will use these fabrics, or if I will use them all or just a few.

Next I add background fabrics and lights that will work with the other fabrics. Again, I don't want everything to match perfectly, but I want to consider whether the choices are light enough in comparison to the darks, so that the animals will be bold enough when added. Or are the fabrics better for use in the filler areas or borders but not for backgrounds behind the animals? I will need some of those filler and border fabrics, too.

Now I actually begin cutting and placing my fabrics. From the lights, I choose which ones will be used as backgrounds and cut them to size. Then I position them on a design wall as they appear in the finished project, leaving spaces between them for the filler areas and inner border. I usually use my favorite background fabric for the largest center background piece and cut the next larger backgrounds from my next favorites. The smaller ones aren't so critical, and are cut last. Keep in mind that if you are using light blue fabrics for only three backgrounds (and say off-white for the rest), evenly or asymmetrically distribute them in the project, so the eye is drawn from one to the other and not all in a row or in one corner.

Next I choose my favorite print fabric and see where in this project I want to use it. If it will be used in some filler areas, sew those filler areas and place them on the design wall. By now I usually have an idea of which fabric I want for the inner border around my 12" center design. I cut and position that, too.

If I like the effect so far, I continue. If not, I take off the offending pieces and replace them with something else. I make up more filler blocks for this project, and place them on the design wall where they belong. I do this until all filler blocks are made, and I am happy with the effect.

Now I decide which fabric I want to use for the animals, flowers, or trees. I sometimes pin a two-inch swatch of fabric on each background to get a better idea of how that particular fabric will look. If I really like a dark fabric for a specific animal, I'll go ahead and follow the fusible web process to trace/fuse/cut the animal out. But I still pin it in place on the background rather than fusing it in place, just in case! Make certain that your dark fabric is bold enough

and all the little curves and angles you cut show up. You don't want to go through all the trouble of cutting out the details of an elk only to have half his antler points disappear into the background!

Now I'm ready to sew the top together. Once the top is complete, I decide on borders. Since the borders on each wallhanging project are so different, I can choose the border as given for this particular project or pick another variation. For this example, I'll go with the project's border. I like to audition fabric for borders, laying out strips of fabric on the design wall around the sewn center. I'm looking to see if the border adds to the project or detracts from it; do I like the width of the border; does the project need another narrow border to accent a particular color, etc. Finally, I think about the binding fabric, again considering whether I want it to be an added bit of color or to smoothly blend into the border fabric. After these decisions are made, I sew!

Color Tips

If you want to darken your fabric a bit, spritz it with cold tea, or tea-dye the complete project. You could also over-dye the completed top with a commercial dye, often done in your washing machine. Always test for colorfastness.

■ If you are auditioning your border fabrics and one seems to really jump at you instead of blending in, more than likely it will *still* be the main focus of the project if chosen. Another common problem is that the fabric is the perfect color but doesn't have enough interest (maybe it's just too simple or plain). You're better off to find another fabric in both cases.

■ The main color tip I can give you is *contrast*. Make sure you have contrast throughout your project and that the silhouettes are bold enough for your taste.

Make It Your Own

Every quilter has a favorite part of the quilting process, whether it is designing a project, selecting fabrics, piecing intricate detailed blocks, paper piecing, appliqué, dimensional work, beading, embroidery, or other embellishment. You can easily make the finished project uniquely your own by incorporating these favorite touches.

I invited a few of my quilting friends with different styles and skill levels to interpret my wallhanging designs in their own way. Each is a specialist in a different area, ranging from miniatures to Celtic work to detailed appliqué to beaded quilted clothing. Quite a variety! The designs they returned were equally varied. You can use their ideas for inspiration and encouragement as you choose how to make your own project.

Here are a few ideas to get your creative juices flowing:

■ Select a design you like and make it as presented, but use animals from another project. Maybe you like the flying geese arrangement used in the bear project, but want moose instead of bears. Change them! Prefer more trees? Fine. Want to combine one of everything? That will work.

■ Again, select a design you like and make it as presented, except change the outer border. Glance at the other projects, find a border that suits your taste, and follow those instructions. Actual length of the borders may vary, so double check your actual measurements.

■ Like a design but want it arranged in its mirror image? That will work too. You may need to draw it out so you don't get confused, but that's easy enough.

■ Select portions of several designs and combine them. Again, you may need to draft out your design on graph paper, but the time it saves will be well worth it! When you're ready to cut out the pieces, remember to add seam allowances to all drawn measurements.

■ Make the project the size given, or add more filler areas or backgrounds to it to make a larger quilt.

■ Select one project and use it as the center medallion for a full-sized quilt. Place it off-center to make an asymmetrical design.

■ Use only the wildlife and foliage designs from this book to combine with other projects.

Little Critters of Creation, 34½" x 30½", 2002, made by Pat Lafky and quilted by Wanda Jeffries, both of Spokane, Washington.

■ Combine techniques. Use fusible web for the animals and trees, traditional piecing for the filler areas and borders, paper piecing for a special section, and add dimensional flowers in another area. What other techniques do you know? What other recent classes have you taken that you want to experiment with? Maybe appliqué a unique vine and flowers over the border to remember a special time of year in your hometown.

■ Embellish with beads, embroidery, silk ribbon embroidery, buttons, cording, yarns, charms, etc. The flower designs would look great with extra embroidery details and some glittery beads in their centers.

■ Add dimensional flowers or butterflies or bugs. Purchase these at your local craft store, or make them yourself. Place them on flowers or trees, or on filler areas and borders.

■ Change the designs to be hand appliquéd. Personally, my appliqué skills aren't good enough for the detail in these designs, so I would have to simplify them before I could appliqué them.

■ Include names and dates in your project somewhere, either in the label or on the surface of your project. This could be to commemorate a visit to a national park, a recent camping trip, a ride you took one weekend, etc.

Basically, I encourage you to each think of a way to make your project uniquely your own. When you hear other quilters say, "I never thought of that!" you know you have succeeded.

Paws in the Woods, 27" x 30", 2002, designed and quilted by Rose Kralik of Newport, Washington.

Roaming Deer, 31½" x 27½", 2002, designed and quilted by Rose Kralik of Newport, Washington.

*My View, 28" x 32½",
2002, by Elaine Pelton
of Sandpoint, Idaho.*

*Vanishing, 21½" x 18½",
2002, by Vicki Costello of
Post Falls, Idaho. Vicki
writes, "After talking
with my friend, Lois
Grutta and seeing what
she learned from a
David Walker class, I
realized this technique
would work for my
background. The ghost-
like silhouettes of the
animals were created by
using window sheer
fabric fused to a light
taupe fabric for a
shadow."*

Finishing Your Project

Borders

There are some general rules of thumb to keep in mind as you select, cut, and sew the borders of your projects.

- **Border width**—I prefer to use my project as my guide. In general, I like to make my border no wider than the size of the majority of the smaller blocks of the project. Since most wall-hangings have a 12" center block with 4" blocks around it, I've chosen to make borders 4" or less. If you plan to do some intricate quilting in the border, that may dictate that it be cut wider to allow for the quilting.

  If you want to include more than one outer border, my favorite method is to make a narrow border framing the project (usually 1" to 2" wide, depending on the size of the project) and then add a wider border. What's your overall impression with the border strips laid next to the project? If it looks good to you, then you've made the right choice. If not, try different widths or different fabrics. Also try fewer or more borders. Remember: Your border(s) should *complement* your project not overpower or detract from it.

- **Border length**—Measure your project through its *center* from top to bottom to determine the length of the side borders. This is the measurement to cut your side borders. I also check the outer edge measurement, and compare. I do this mostly to see how accurate I am and to see how much easing I have to do to make the borders fit. If the measurements near the edges of my project are much different from the center ones, I will look to see where I can adjust my top or fudge a little on the length of the borders. Pin this border RST with your project top: pin at each end of the border piece, at its center point, and in between as much as you need to be comfortable. Sew accurately and ease any excess fabric into the seam as you sew. Press, generally toward the your border. Repeat this process for the top and bottom of your quilt, measuring through the quilt's center from side to side.

- **What border to sew first**—top and bottom or sides? There's always a lot of confusion about which border to add first to your finished quilt top. Take a look at your project and be consistent. If inner side borders were added first, then any other side borders should be added before the top and bottom borders. The wallhangings in this book are shown with the sides added first, and then the top and bottom borders are added. This was followed for both the narrow inner border around the center 12" square, and for the outer border (where applicable). Whatever your preference, be consistent throughout your project.

  After all borders are added, confirm that the top is still square and make corrections if needed. One of the easiest ways is to set a large square ruler (like a 15" square) in the corner, and look at where the lines on the ruler align with seams on the top. Are they consistently in the same place? Make adjustments by taking bigger seams if necessary or trimming away excess border fabric.

Quilting Designs

How and how much you choose to quilt your project is definitely a personal decision. Make that decision based on your particular situation, to fit your needs, style, and skill level. First, ask yourself these questions, and use the answers to make your quilting choices:

◼ What is the purpose of this quilt?

◼ How will it be used or displayed?

◼ Will it be washed and handled a lot?

◼ Do I want one area of the quilt to be more dominant than another?

◼ What is my skill level, and how comfortable am I with machine or hand quilting?

My preference for batting for wallhangings is Warm & Natural. For full-size quilts and lap quilts, I prefer Hobbs Heirloom 80/20.

Naturally you will put more thought into the quilting designs for a quilt that you'd like to enter in a quilt show than you would put into a baby quilt. The batting you choose may be different, as well as the amount and detail of quilting done. From experience, I can tell you that the amount of quilting you do on a project will change as your experience level changes. When I first started machine quilting, I was happy to stitch in the ditch around the main parts of a project and leave the rest alone. Now I enjoy playing with different filler stitches like stippling and loopty-loops. Most of my projects are quilted heavily, with stitching closer than 2" apart.

For most of the wallhanging projects shown, I have machine quilted in-the-ditch around both sides of the framing of the 12" center blocks and in the seam area between the wallhanging and its outer border. I stitch with free motion directly on the animals, trees, mountains, and other fused elements, following the shape and stitching about ⅛" inside the raw edge. This anchors the elements securely, especially since most of my projects travel and are handled a lot. A variety of filler stitches are used to quilt the empty areas between blocks. I have chosen to quilt something specific in the pieced areas, like the flying geese units and checkerboards, and the outer borders.

Following is a table showing several different quilting designs to get you started, but don't be limited by them! Use your imagination and experiment to find others. In addition to these designs, consider using the animal, plant, and tree diagrams at the back of the book as inspiration.

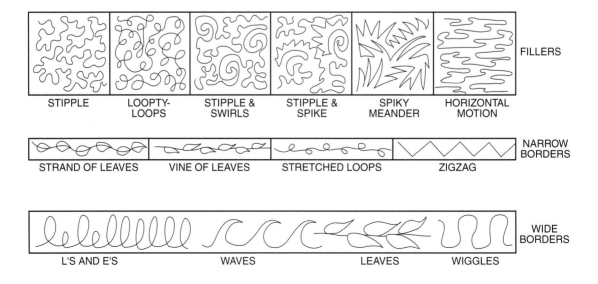

| STIPPLE | LOOPTY-LOOPS | STIPPLE & SWIRLS | STIPPLE & SPIKE | SPIKY MEANDER | HORIZONTAL MOTION | FILLERS |

| STRAND OF LEAVES | VINE OF LEAVES | STRETCHED LOOPS | ZIGZAG | NARROW BORDERS |

| L'S AND E'S | WAVES | LEAVES | WIGGLES | WIDE BORDERS |

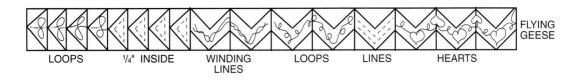

FLYING GEESE

LOOPS   ¼" INSIDE   WINDING LINES   LOOPS   LINES   HEARTS

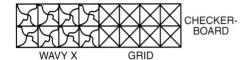

CHECKER-BOARD

WAVY X   GRID

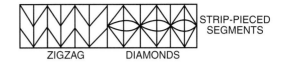

STRIP-PIECED SEGMENTS

ZIGZAG   DIAMONDS

Layering & Quilting

1. Press your completed project and the backing (sometimes called the lining) you have chosen.

2. Confirm that your quilt top is square. Correct it if it isn't.

3. Decide how you will quilt your project. Mark these lines now if necessary, using your favorite method. I suggest testing your marking methods to make sure they will remain visible long enough for you to quilt the project, yet be easily removed once the project is complete.

4. Cut backing and batting about 4" larger than the size of your wall hanging project (cut 10" larger for twin and full-sized quilts).

5. Stretch the backing on a flat surface, WSU. For wallhangings, I do this on my table or dining room floor. Tape the edges down at roughly four-inch intervals, keeping the backing flat and taut, but not over-stretched. For larger projects, use a large floor or push two conference tables together. Use tape, clamps, clips, or whatever you find that works to hold this backing in place. Remove any lint or foreign objects from the surface.

6. Center and smooth the batting over the backing, again removing any lint or foreign objects from the surface. This is not pinned in place or taped down.

7. Center and smooth the pressed quilt top, RSU, over the batting.

8. Pin baste, baste with a basting tool, or baste with thread. Begin in the center and work outward, basting approximately every 2" to 3", depending on the type of batting used. If you are thread basting, use a light-colored thread to ensure that you don't leave residue from basting thread on your quilt. Take small enough stitches so you won't catch the loose thread as you quilt, yet long enough to be easily removed.

9. Remove tape, clamps, clips, etc.

10. Quilt by hand or machine, again beginning in the center and working outward.

11. Remove any remaining basting pins or thread.

12. Square up the quilted project, trimming the backing and batting to size.

Binding

My favorite binding method is a double-fold technique, beginning with 2¼" strips cut on the cross-grain. Most quilters use 2½" strips, so I have based yardage amounts for binding on the wider strips. Another area where my process may vary from yours is that I generally overlap the ends of the binding rather than connect them. Consult other quilt books for other options. Directions for my method follow:.

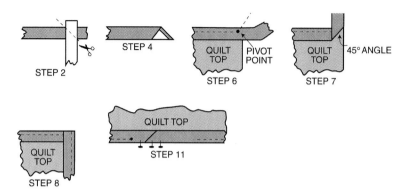

1. Cut enough strips, selvage to selvage, to go around your wallhanging or quilt plus about 8".

2. Sew the strips together at a 45-degree angle. RST Trim the seams to ¼" and press open.

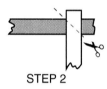

STEP 2

3. Press the long binding strip in half WST, so it is approximately 1¼" wide.

4. Cut one end at a 45-degree angle. Press ¼" under to finish the edge. This is your beginning edge.

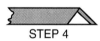

STEP 4

5. Place the beginning edge of your binding on the quilt top at the center bottom (or at an inconspicuous spot), RST and raw edges even. Begin sewing through all layers approximately 3" from this point, using ¼" seam and backstitching.

6. Sew to ¼" from the first corner. Pivot with the needle down at this point, and continue sewing out at a 45-degree angle to the corner of the quilt. Clip threads, and remove the quilt from the machine (no backstitching).

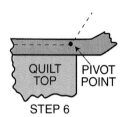

STEP 6

7. Fold the binding away from you, as in the diagram. The 45-degree angle sewn will help you fold this correctly.

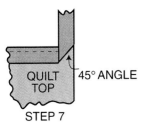

8. Fold the binding down toward you, aligning the top edge of the folded binding with the top edge of your quilt. The raw edges of the binding and right side of the quilt top should align.

9. Sew ¼" seam, continuing to the next corner.

10. Repeat Steps 6 to 9 until you have completed all four corners.

11. Trim excess binding to ½" longer than the furthest point of your beginning binding. Pin in place, tucking the end inside the angled finished edge where you began.

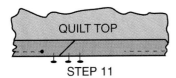

12. Sew using ¼" seam, backstitching over your beginning stitches.

13. Fold the binding to the back of the quilt, stitching in place by hand using a blind stitch.

Sleeve & Label

I like to sew a sleeve to all my wallhangings so it's there when I need it. The best time to do this is after the binding is machine sewn to the quilt, but before it is hand stitched down.

Sleeve—Cut a 6" wide strip of fabric that matches or coordinates with the quilt back. Cut it about 1½" narrower than the width of the finished project. Turn ¼" under on each short side, pressing to finish the raw edges. Fold the strip in half along the length, wrong sides together. Press. Place it on the back of the wallhanging, centering it width-wise and aligning the raw edges with the upper edge of the quilt. Sew through all layers, being careful not to catch the turned edge of the binding at the outer edges. You will be sewing through the sleeve, quilt, and binding—on the same stitching line as the binding. The upper edge will be caught in your hand stitching as you turn and sew the binding down. Use a blind stitch to sew the folded edge down by hand.

Label—Plan to add a label to your quilt. This is a great way for you to remember details about the quilt and why you made it, plus it adds a loving touch when it is made as a gift for a friend or relative. Include on the label the name of the quilt or quilt pattern, date, occasion, your name and city/state, and any other details that are appropriate. I made a special label on a quilt I gave to a dear elderly friend who was in a nursing home. When she died, her children were honored to take this quilt to their home, in memory of both their mother and me.

For Teachers Only

I teach quilting classes regularly, and I'm always looking for a good book that I can easily teach from, one that is worth the cost and is a reference book that my students would be willing to add to their library. For that reason, I've put together some class ideas here to make your life as a quilting teacher a little easier!

There are several class possibilities in this book. Thumb through the section on piecing techniques, and see what your students are asking you to teach them. Then look at my class suggestions, and modify them to fit your needs and the skill level of your students.

Class Idea 1: Pillow

Class length: 4 hours

Skill level: Beginner

> **Tip:** Make up kits for the pillow, and include the kit in the cost of the class. Offer as a children's class or as a class for parent and child.

Class description—Learn how to use fusible web as you make a charming pillow. Students choose which forest animal or scene to add to their pillow top, and they construct the pillow in class. Beginners welcome, book required.

Class focus—Each 12" center square of the wallhanging projects in Chapter 3 can be made into a pillow, or encourage students to design their own pillow top using the elements provided in Chapter 5, The Designs. Focus is on learning the fusible web technique, finishing options, and completing the pillow.

Class outline

A. Introductions of students and teacher. Teacher tells students what to expect from the class.

B. Show different fusible web samples, on the bolt if possible. Let students feel them.

C. Show projects or samples using different webs, if you have them.

D. Reference Chapter 1, Using Fusible Web and Fusible Web Tips.

E. Demonstrate using webs—tracing, cutting, and fusing.

F. Help students with color choices.

G. Students trace designs. Fuse designs in place (or pin in place on backgrounds).

H. Pillow construction. (Follow directions for pillow projects in Chapter 4.)

A Forest of Quilts ◆ 39

Class Idea 2:

Wallhanging, Chosen By Teacher

Class length: 2 to 3 classes, 4 hours each

Skill level: Confident beginner to intermediate

Class description—Make a wonderful wallhanging for your cabin in the woods, as you learn new piecing techniques and how to use fusible webs. Confident beginners welcome, book required.

Class focus—Teacher selects project that will challenge students. If students are ready to learn how to make flying geese, perhaps select the Moose or Bear wallhanging as your project. For a more in-depth class, select The Challenge wallhanging, which has several different techniques in the filler units. Teach one or two piecing techniques per class, depending on the class length and student skill level. Encourage students to square up the filler units before sewing the top together. Sizes of each unit are listed with their cutting or piecing directions. Allow enough time for students to reach the top construction phase. Help them measure for and add borders.

Class outline

A. Introductions of students and teacher. Teacher tells students what to expect from the class each day; students share their expectations.

B. Show different fusible web samples, on the bolt if possible. Let students feel them.

C. Show projects or samples using different webs, if you have them.

D. Reference Chapter 1, Using Fusible Web and Fusible Web Tips.

E. Demonstrate using webs—tracing, cutting, and fusing.

F. Help students with color choices for their project. Reference Chapter 2, Beginning Your Project and Fabric Selection.

G. Students trace, cut, and fuse designs in place; or pin in place on backgrounds.

First class probably ends here.

H. Filler unit instruction. Reference Chapter 1, Techniques. Follow instructions for each pertinent technique, demonstrating each or having a sample at different stages of completion for the students to see.

I. Demonstrate how to square up each filler unit, encouraging students to be accurate with their piecing and pressing.

J. Demonstrate placing filler units and background pieces on a design wall and how to audition different fabric and color choices.

Depending on how many filler techniques are in the project, second class ends here.

K. Reference Chapter 2, Make It Your Own, and encourage students to personalize their wallhanging.

L. Reference Chapter 2, Finishing Your Project, for specifics on borders, layering, quilting, binding, and labeling the finished wallhanging. Borders are a great point to focus on. Show the students how to accurately measure for and add them.

The Challenge, 38" x 26", 2002, made by Fonda L. Sarft, Kootenai, Idaho.

Class Idea 3:

Wallhanging, Design Your Own

Class length: 2 to 3 classes, 4 hours each

Skill level: Very confident beginners, intermediate to advanced

Class description—Design it yourself! Using the many wallhangings in the book as a starting point, students will branch off to design the layout and filler units of their own wallhanging. Students will learn balance in design and color, and speed piecing methods to sew the project together. Confident beginners welcome, book required.

Class focus—Encourage your students to spread their quilting wings and explore the unknown in designing. Assume that most are unfamiliar with drafting quilt blocks and most don't like math. Focus on design, color, and balance. Encourage students to make their project unique, choosing their favorite pieced elements and animal designs from those provided—or include others! Help with drawing their design on graph paper. Then work with them on color placement. You may be able to skip some instruction on fusible web or the speed piecing techniques if they are already familiar with them. The key in this class is to *encourage* your students to step beyond their comfort zone and grow as quilters.

Class outline

A. Introductions of students and teacher. Teacher tells students what to expect from the class each day; students share expectations and anxieties.

B. Browse through book, *A Forest of Quilts*, with students. Look closely at the wallhangings in Chapter 3. Have students make a list of what animal(s), trees, filler units, etc. they want to include in their projects, separating the favorites from the maybes.

C. On graph paper, have students begin their design by drawing their 12" center square and the 1" frame around it. Next, draw the approximate outer edge of the wallhanging, considering the final dimensions and symmetry desired. This is approximate, and just a guideline.

D. Students pencil in the approximate placement of their background areas, to accommodate the designs they want to include (trees, tracks, flowers, etc.). Explain what makes a design balanced, and help students achieve this balance in their layout.

E. Students pencil in their favorite filler pieces, again keeping the design balanced. (Color will be considered later.)

F. Continue with this process until the complete wallhanging is drawn out and the project looks feasible. Consider ease of sewing the new design compared to the skill level of the quilter. If it would make more sense to have the blocks twice the size originally drawn, or moved one inch over, modify the design.

First class would probably end here.

G. Review final designs of each student in front of the class; learn from each other.

Eagles in Flight, 28½" x 32½", 2002, made by Sally Clouse, Coeur d'Alene, Idaho.

H. Talk about color choices, contrast, and show combinations that work well. Review the fabrics students plan to use, and confirm they are acceptable. Reference Chapter 2, Beginning Your Project and Fabric Selection. Show the students how to audition fabrics on a design wall, and talk about balancing color.

I. Determine what filler units will be made by the students. Demonstrate the appropriate speedy techniques as given in Chapter 1. Encourage students to square up the units to the proper size before moving on.

J. Have students make up several filler units and place them on the design wall with their background fabrics.

K. Talk about fusible web products and review that process with students. Show different fusible web samples, on the bolt if possible. Let students feel them. Reference Chapter 1, Using Fusible Web and Fusible Web Tips. Demonstrate using webs if needed—tracing, cutting, and fusing.

L. Again talk about color choices in reference to the fusible web designs, suggesting that students audition the fabric by placing it on the design wall in the proper position. Talk again about color balance.

M. Students trace designs. Cut out designs, and fuse in place.

N. Reference Chapter 2, Make It Your Own, and talk about ways students could personalize their wallhanging.

O. Reference Chapter 2, Finishing Your Project, for specifics on borders, layering, quilting, binding, and labeling the finished wallhanging.

P. Talk about where students can go from here with their new-found design experience.

Little Critters of Creation, 34½" x 30½", 2002, made by Pat Lafky and quilted by Wanda Jeffries, both of Spokane, Washington.

Class Idea 4:

Two Square

Class length: 1 to 2 classes, 6 to 8 hours total

Skill level: Confident beginner

Tip: Another candidate to be made up in kits and sold separately from class.

Class description—Choose your favorite novelty print and two contrasting fabrics. Add speed piecing techniques, straight seams, and lots of repetition, and what do you get? A first quilt, a wonderful baby gift, or a dorm quilt—all with your favorite fabrics! Beginners with rotary cutting experience welcome, book required.

Class focus—This is a fast project, teaching speed piecing techniques with lots of repetition. Students should come to class with their fabrics already chosen and cut, ready to learn some quick ways to sew this project together. Encourage accurate ¼" seams and good pressing.

Class outline

A. Introductions of students and teacher. Teacher tells students what to expect from the class.

B. Share with students all samples made up from this pattern, the Nine Patch, the quilt, the pillow, or the pillow case. Inexperienced quilters may prefer to make a smaller project first.

C. Reference Chapter 4, Two Square projects, for cutting and piecing instructions.

D. Show students some fabric combinations that you have chosen for the project that would be acceptable. Review the fabric choices of students and confirm that contrasting fabrics will show up well against novelty prints.

E. Demonstrate how to fussy cut novelty prints, and explain strip piecing and cutting segments to length.

F. Students fussy cut their novelty prints. Place on a design wall.

G. Students sew the strips together and re-cut them as directed in project instructions. Help students place the strip units around the novelty prints on their design wall.

First class would probably end here.

H. Talk about top construction, row by row.

I. Students sew their top together.

J. Demonstrate how to square up the top, measure and add borders, referencing Chapter 2, Finishing Your Project. Talk about preparing the quilt top for quilting. Again, reference Chapter 2, Finishing Your Project, for binding instructions and ideas on labels.

CHAPTER 3
Wallhangings

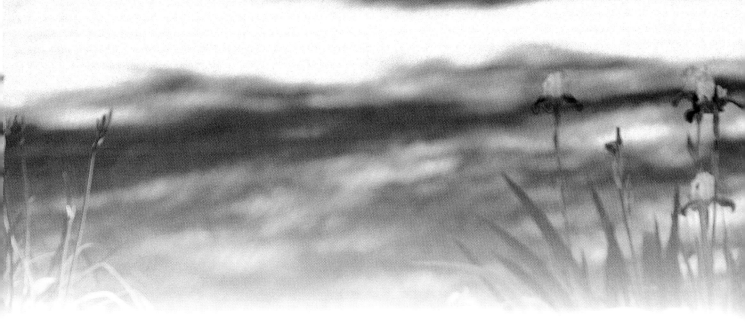

Fabrics & Yardage

As you look at the directions for your project, notice that I've listed the yardage needed for every element in the wallhanging. I've done this for two reasons: First, if you have a good stash of fabric and only need to purchase one or two of the larger pieces, you have the information right there. Amounts needed for scraps will vary depending on the size of your scraps, so use the amounts given as a guide. For those of you with no stash, all the fabrics and yardages needed are listed.

One last comment on fabrics: Yardage amounts are estimates, based on at least 40" usable width of fabric, unless told otherwise. Remember to pre-wash all fabrics and use the highest quality 100% cotton for best results.

General Construction

1. After settling on colors and specific fabrics (reference Chapter 2, Beginning Your Project), place the background fabrics on your design wall, following the layout diagram of your project.

2. Place the inner border on your design wall around the center square.

3. Sew the filler pieces for your project. Verify that your filler pieces measure the same as listed in your directions. If they don't, take wider or narrower seams or press better to reach the correct measurements. Place the filler pieces on the design wall. If you're unhappy with fabrics or color combinations, make new filler pieces and replace. Once you're satisfied with the filler pieces, continue.

4. Audition the fabrics for your design—the animals, trees, birds, flowers, etc. Place a 2" to 3" swatch of the selected fabrics on their respective backgrounds. Once you're satisfied with your choices, continue.

5. Fuse the designs to the background pieces.

6. Sew the top together. First, sew the inner border to your center square or rectangle, sides first, then top and bottom. Next, look at the Construction Diagram to determine what elements make up each larger chunk. Sew these elements together to form the numbered chunks. Sew the chunks together, following the number sequence.

7. Refer to Chapter 2 for ideas on how to make your project your own; how to measure for and add borders; how to layer, baste, quilt, bind, and add a sleeve and label to your project; and for specific quilting ideas. For the majority of these wallhangings, I have quilted in the ditch around the center block and borders. I did a free motion quilting stitch on all animals and trees, about ⅛" inside from the raw edges. I used a variety of filler stitches and designs in borders. See the diagram of quilting stitches in Chapter 2, Finishing Your Project.

Teachers! Look in Chapter 2, For Teachers Only, to find complete outlines for teaching two different classes based on these wallhangings. One class focuses on learning the speedy techniques in a specific wallhanging. The other class focuses on helping students design their own wallhanging. You'll find newsletter descriptions, information on the focus of each class, plus complete outlines to teach from. Choose the class that best fits the skill level of your students!

Disappearing Moose

by Terrie Kralik, 2002

Special Note:

The full-sized moose couldn't be drawn on one page, so it has been drawn in two parts in the pattern section (Chapter 5, The Designs) with jagged edges showing how to align the two pieces. When tracing the moose onto your fusible web, trace one part, reposition your fusible web and align the jagged edge with the remaining part of the moose, and continue tracing. When complete, your moose will be traced as a single piece. Disregard your drawn jagged lines in the middle of the moose when you cut out the fabric. (You can trace the moose onto a larger piece of paper, so you can see exactly how big it is as a whole. Keep this with your design pages for future projects.)

Position the land strip behind the moose somewhere above the center line of the background square. I prefer to place the land below the antlers, so the details of the antlers show completely. Play with this horizon line until you find what fits your taste.

Yardage Needed

Center block background—fat
   quarter
6 backgrounds—¼ yd
Flying geese & strip units
   Light—¼ yd
   Medium—⅛ yd
   Dark—¼ yd
Inner border—⅛ yd
Outer Border—⅓ yd
Moose, tracks, tree trunks—
   ⅓ yd
Trees, land—⅛ yd
Quilt back—1 yd
Batting—28" x 32"
Binding—⅓ yd
Fusible web—1 yd

Do you know how easily moose blend into their natural surroundings? You wouldn't think they could just disappear into a grove of trees, until you witness it for yourself. In fabric, you can choose the right fabrics and make sure your moose are easily seen. Add flying geese, strip-sewn pieces, and a narrow border and you have this wallhanging!

Finished size: 26½" x 30"

Cut

Background fabrics
—cut one each
A—12½" x 12½"
B—4½" x 6½"
C—6½" x 4½"
D—4½" x 10½"
E—8½" x 4½"
F—10½" x 5½"
G—4½" x 8½"

Inner Border
H—1½" x 12½", cut 2
I—1½" x 14½", cut 2

Outer Border
J—2½" x 26½", cut 2
K—2½" x 26½", cut 2

Binding
2½" wide strips, cut 4

Filler Pieces

Flying Geese units

Use the Fast Flying Geese technique:

- Make 16 units, one is excess, 2½" x 4½" (unfinished size).

Dark—5¼" squares, cut 4
Light—2⅞" squares, cut 16

Strip-Pieced unit

Use the Strip-Pieced Border technique:

- Make 1 unit 3½" x 10½" and 1 unit 4½" x 6½" (unfinished sizes).

Dark and/or medium—1½" x 9", cut 10 total

1. Sew strips together along the 9" side. Press all in one direction.

2. Cross cut into one 3½" segment and one 4½" segment.

3. Cut or rip out seams to reach the proper length on the 4½" section. Verify that the 3½" section is 10½" wide; make corrections or trim if necessary.

Construction and Quilting

Refer to the beginning of the chapter for General Construction directions. See Chapter 2, Finishing Your Project, for specific quilting diagrams. This project was quilted with a double diagonal line behind all designs on light background pieces, and with loopty-loops and a zigzag or diamond pattern in other areas.

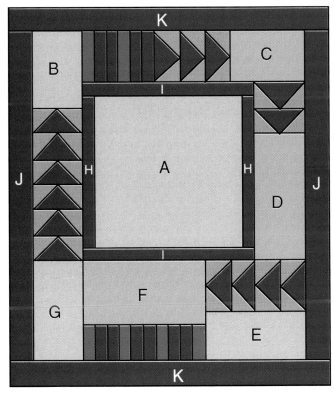

Layout Diagram

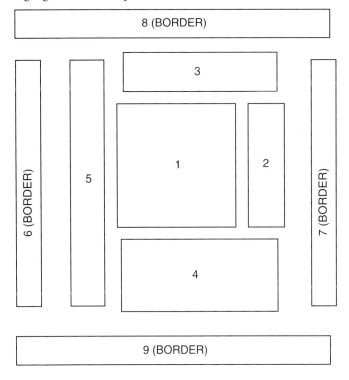

Construction Diagram

Tread Lightly
by Terrie Kralik, 2002

Wild deer are so elusive, you seldom see much more than a glimpse of a tail or legs as they dash into the woods. This design has captured them so they won't get away, and it includes the sheds they leave behind (their antlers), some of the vegetation they might eat, and the trees that make up their home.

Special Note:

Make the horizon line in the center Block A by cutting a strip of fusible web ½" x 13" and fuse it to the *ground* fabric. Cut a piece from this measuring ⅜" x 12½". Trim the upper edge only to give it a gentle curve so it looks like a ridge or hill in the distance. Use your ruler to place this 5¼" from the lower raw edge of the block. It will extend to the edge of your background fabric, and be sewn into the side seams. Or, try placing this in different positions to find what you like best.

The flower in this project can be made in two parts to add color to the flower, if desired. Just trace the flower and the stem/leaves separately, fuse to the appropriate fabrics, and continue.

Yardage Needed

Center block background—fat quarter
6 backgrounds—¼ yd
Outer pieced border, checkerboards, strip units
    Medium—½ yd
    Dark—½ yd
Inner border—⅛ yd
Deer, sheds (antlers), tracks—¼ yd
Trees, flower—⅛ yd
Quilt back—1 yd
Batting—30" x 34"
Binding—⅓ yd
Fusible web—1 yd

Finished size: 28½" x 32½"

Cut

Background Fabrics—cut one each	Inner Border
A—12½" x 12½"	H—1½" x 12½", cut 2
B—4½" x 6½"	I—1½" x 14½", cut 2
C—6½" x 4½"	
D—4½" x 8½"	Outer Border
E—4½" x 4½"	J—2" x 26½", cut 2 light and 2 dark
F—10½" x 5½"	K—2" x 22½", cut 2 light and 2 dark
G—4½" x 8½"	
	Binding
	2½" wide strips, cut 4

Filler Pieces

Four Patch units

Use the Checkerboard technique:

• Make 9 units 4½" square (unfinished size).

Dark—2½" strip, selvage to selvage
　　　—2½" x 6" strip
Light—2½" strip, selvage to selvage
　　　—2½" x 6" strip

1. Sew full length dark + light strips together. Sew 6" dark + light strips together. Press seams to the dark.

2. Re-cut into 2½" segments, making 18 segments.

3. Sew into nine Four Patch units.

• Make 4 units 3½" square (unfinished size).

Dark—2" x 18" strip
Light—2" x 18" strip
1. Sew strips together. Press seams to the dark.

2. Re-cut into 2" segments, making eight segments.

3. Sew into four Four Patch units.

Strip-Pieced units

Use the Strip-Pieced Border technique:

• Make 1 Strip Pieced unit 4½" x 6½" and 1 Strip Pieced unit 3½" x 10½" (unfinished size).

Dark—1½" x 18" strip
　　　—1½" x 7" strip
Light (or medium)—1½" x 18" strips, cut 2

1. Sew 18" long strips together, along the 18" side—light + dark + light. Press all in one direction. Cut one segment 3½" x 10½".

2. Sew a 7" dark strip to the remaining segment. Press all in one direction. Cut one segment 4½" x 6½".

Construction and Quilting

Refer to the beginning of the chapter for General Construction directions. See Chapter 2, Finishing Your Project, for specific quilting diagrams. This project was quilted with loopty-loops, a stipple, swirls, and a wavy X

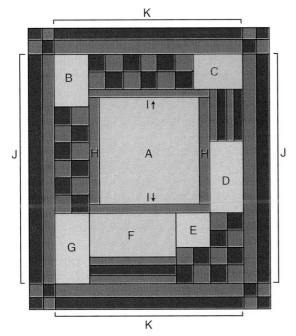

Layout Diagram

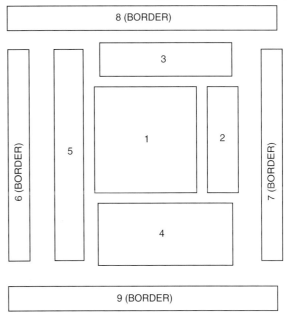

Construction Diagram

Bear Collage

by Terrie Kralik, 2002

Special Note:

Each of the tree trunks can be traced individually, or the two that overlap can be traced as a single tree to make alignment simpler. Since the full-sized trees couldn't be drawn on one page, they have been shown in parts in the pattern section, with jagged edges showing how to align the pieces. When tracing them onto your fusible web, trace one part, reposition your fusible web and align the jagged edge with the remaining part of the same tree, and continue tracing. When complete, your tree will be traced as a single piece. Disregard your drawn jagged lines in the middle of the tree when you cut out the piece.

The paw print is shown in Chapter 5, The Designs, facing two directions. Trace the one that looks like the right-hand paw, and use the other drawing as a guideline for laying out the pieces on your background fabric. The smaller parts of the print can be drawn with a permanent marking pen or sewn with embroidery stitches instead of making them with fusible web.

Yardage Needed

Center block background—fat
    quarter
4 backgrounds and 4 filler
    rectangles—¼ yd
Flying geese
        Medium—⅓ yd
        Dark—⅓ yd
Bear, trees, paw print, leaf—
    ¼ yd
Inner border—⅛ yd
Outer border—½ yd
Quilt back—1 yd
Batting—30" x 34"
Binding—⅓ yd
Fusible web—1 yd

Be careful in the woods when bears are out. They really don't like to be surprised (and the feeling is mutual)! This wallhanging captures the curiosity and attitude of bears as they wander through the forest. Give them the respect and space they need, and we can all get along just fine.

Finished size: 28" x 32"

Cut

Background Fabrics—cut one each
A—12½" x 12½"
B—4½" x 4 ½"
C—4½" x 8½"
D—12" x 4½"
E—3" x 4½"

Filler Fabric (print fabric)
F—2½" x 4½", cut 4

Inner Border
G—1½" x 12½", cut 2
H—1½" x 14½", cut 2

Outer Border
I—3½" x 26½", cut 2
J—3½" x 28½", cut 2

Binding
2½" wide strips, cut 4

Filler Pieces

Flying Geese units

Use the Fast Flying Geese technique:

• Make 16 units, one is excess, 2½" x 4½" (unfinished size).

Dark—5¼" squares, cut 4
Light—2⅞" squares, cut 16

• Make 16 units, one is excess, 2½" x 4½" (unfinished size).

Dark—2⅞" squares, cut 16
Light—5¼" squares, cut 4

Construction and Quilting

Refer to the beginning of the chapter for General Construction directions. See Chapter 2, Finishing Your Project, for specific quilting diagrams. This project was quilted with winding lines, zigzags, loopty-loops, stipples, and spikes.

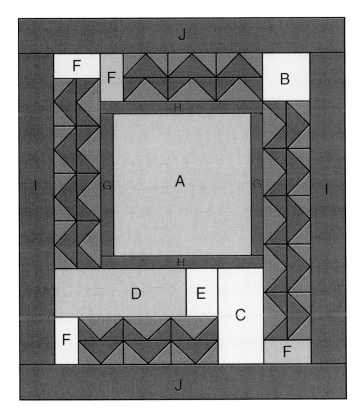

Layout Diagram

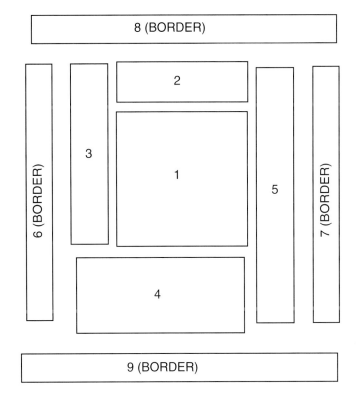

Construction Diagram

Barbara has machine quilted lines to define the wings and veins on the leaves. She has quilted branches and leaves in the filler areas.

Yardage Needed

Center block background—fat quarter
4 backgrounds and 4 filler rectangles—¼ yd
Flying geese
    Medium—⅓ yd
    Dark—⅓ yd
Inner border—⅛ yd
Outer border—½ yd
Green leafy tree—¼ yd
Brown trees and branches—¼ yd
Blue for birds—⅛ yd
Quilt back—1 yd
Batting—29" x 33"
Binding—⅓ yd
Fusible web—1 yd

Bluebirds Forever

Designed and created by Barbara Lambrecht of Chattaroy, Washington, 2002

Barbara's design uses the same layout as the Bear Collage project and the leafy tree section from the center block of the Majestic Elk wallhanging. She has added her own drawings of Western Bluebirds in their natural habitat and added great detail with machine quilting.

Finished size: approx. 27½" x 31"

Cut

Background Fabrics—cut one each	Inner Border
A—12½" x 12½"	G—1½" x 12½", cut 2
B—4½" x 4½"	H—1½" x 14½", cut 2
C—4½" x 8½"	
D—12" x 4½"	Outer Border
E—3" x 4½"	I—3½" x 26½", cut 2
	J—3½" x 28½", cut 2
Filler Fabric (print fabric)	Binding
F—2½" x 4½", cut 4	2½" wide strips, cut 4

Filler Pieces

Flying Geese units

Use the Fast Flying Geese technique:

- Make 16 units, one is excess, 2½" x 4½" (unfinished size).

Dark—5¼" squares, cut 4
Light—2⅞" squares, cut 16

- Make 16 units, one is excess, 2½" x 4½" (unfinished size).

Dark—2⅞" squares, cut 16
Light—5¼" squares, cut 4

Construction and Quilting

Refer to the beginning of the chapter for General Construction directions. See Chapter 2, Finishing Your Project, for specific quilting diagrams. This project was quilted with winding lines, zigzags, loopty-loops, stipples, and spikes.

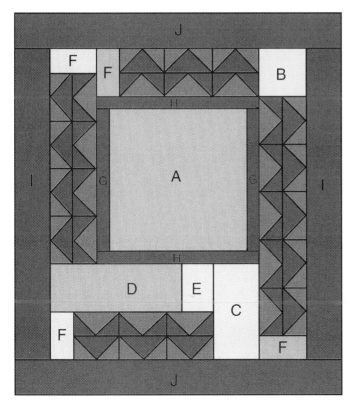

Layout Diagram

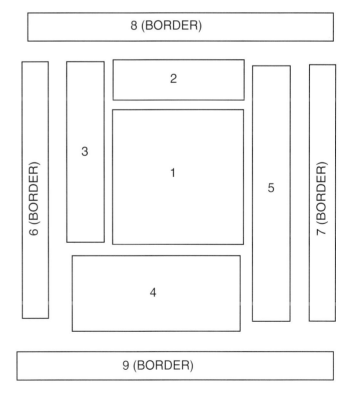

Construction Diagram

Majestic Elk

by Terrie Kralik, 2002

Special Note:

The leaf on this design is from the Bear Collage. Notice that the foliage of the center block extends to the raw edge of the background fabric, and should be fused in place before adding borders to it.

Yardage Needed

Center block background—fat quarter
8 backgrounds—¼ yd
Half-square triangles and strip units
    Medium—¼ yd
    Dark—¼ yd
Inner border—⅛ yd
Outer border
    Medium—⅛ yd
    Dark—½ yd
Quilt back—1 yd
Batting—30" x 34"
Binding—⅓ yd
Fusible web—1 yd

Elk are often described as majestic and regal, and their antlers are very unique. Just imagine trying to walk through a dense forest carrying a pair of their antlers! I'm still not sure how they can manage with little problem.

Finished size: 28½" x 32"

Cut

Background Fabrics	H—1½" x 14½", cut 2
A—12½" x 12½", cut 1	Outer border
B—4½" x 4½", cut 4	I—3½" x 26½", cut 2
C—4½" x 10½", cut 1	J—3½" x 22½", cut 2
D—10½" x 4½", cut 1	K—3½" x 3½", cut 4 (corner
E—4½" x 8½", cut 1	posts)
F—6½" x 4½", cut 1	
	Binding
Inner Border	2½" wide strips, cut 4
G—1½" x 12½", cut 2	

Filler Pieces

Half-Square Triangles

Use the Half-Square Triangle technique:

• Make 22 units 2½" square (unfinished size).

Medium—2⅞" strip, selvage to selvage
Dark—2⅞" strip, selvage to selvage

Re-cut each strip into 11 squares, 2⅞".

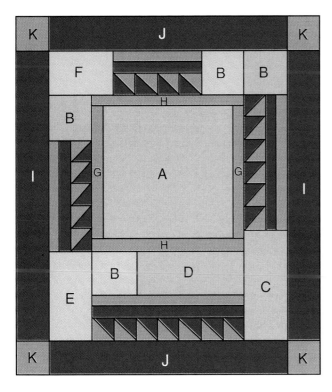

Layout Diagram

Strip-Pieced unit

Use the Strip-Pieced Border technique:

• Make one section each of these lengths (unfinished size):

2½" x 14½"
2½" x 12½"
2½" x 10½"
2½" x 8½"
Medium—1½" wide strip, selvage to selvage
    —1½" x 10" strip
Dark—1½" wide strip, selvage to selvage
    —1½" x 10" strip

1. Sew along the length of the strips, one medium plus one dark of the same length. Press seams toward the dark.

2. Cut the segments into the lengths listed.

Construction and Quilting

Refer to the beginning of the chapter for General Construction directions. See Chapter 2, Finishing Your Project, for specific quilting diagrams. This project was quilted with a stipple, stipple and swirls, and strand of leaves.

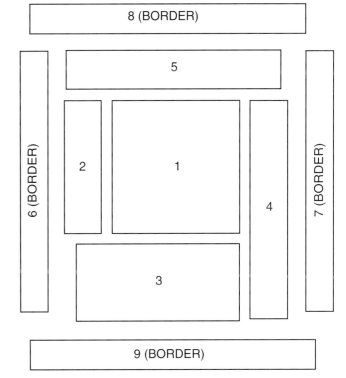

Construction Diagram

The Challenge

By Fonda L. Sarff of Kootenai, Idaho, 2002

Yardage Needed

Light backgrounds, center
  rectangle, filler pieces—1⅛ yd
Both dark borders, filler
  pieces—1 yd
Elk, tracks, tree, leaf—⅓ yd
Quilt back—1¼ yd
Batting—40" x 28"
Binding—⅓ yd
Fusible web—¾ yd

This project combines several different techniques for filler areas. Choose three fabrics, or combine scraps of three colors to be just as effective. Note that Fonda has drawn the small circles of each elk track using a permanent marking pen rather than making them with fabric and fusible web.

The standing elk, elk tracks, and tree are from the Majestic Elk project; the leaf is from the Flora & Fauna project. The fighting elk is unique to this project and is found in Chapter 5, The Designs.

Finished size: approx. 38" x 26"

Cut

Background fabrics	Outer Border
A—24½" x 12½", cut 1	F—2½" x 22½", cut 2
B—14½" x 4½", cut 2	G—2½" x 38½", cut 2
C—4½" x 6½", cut 2	Binding
Inner Border	2½" wide strips, cut 4
D—1½" x 12½", cut 2	
E—1½" x 26½", cut 2	

Filler Pieces

Half-Square Triangles

Use the Half-Square Triangle technique:

• Make 6 units 2½" square (unfinished size).

Light—2⅞" squares, cut 3
Dark—2⅞" squares, cut 3

Flying Geese units

Use the Fast Flying Geese technique:

• Make 12 units, one is excess, 2½" x 4½" (unfinished size).

Dark—5¼" squares, cut 3
Light—2⅞" squares, cut 12

• Make 4, one is excess, 2½" x 4½" (unfinished size).

Dark—2⅞" squares, cut 4
Light—5¼" square, cut 1

Four Patch units

Use the Checkerboard technique:

• Make 4 units 4½" square (unfinished size).

Light—2½" x 22"
Dark—2½" x 22"

Re-cut into 2½" segments

Strip-Pieced unit

Use the Strip-Pieced Border technique:

• Make one unit 2½" x 12½" (unfinished size).

Light—1½" x 12½"
Dark—1½" x 12½"

Construction and Quilting

Construction for this project is a little different than the others, starting with a partial seam. After fusing your designs in place, sew the pieces together to form the large numbered chunks of your project. See the Construction Diagram.

1. Sew Section 1 and Section 2, beginning at the lower edge. Stop stitching about 2" from the upper edge of Section 1.

2. Add Sections 3, 4, and 5 as usual. Now you can finish the first seam. Add borders in order as shown. Refer to Chapter 2, Finishing Your Project, for specific quilting diagrams.

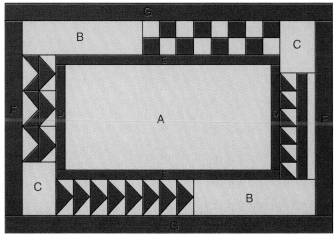

Layout Diagram

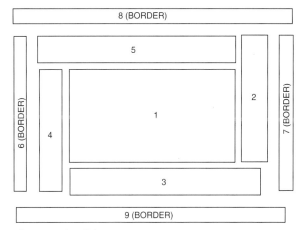

Construction Diagram

Patriotic Eagle

by Terrie Kralik, 2002

Yardage Needed

Center block background—fat quarter
Red—⅓ yd
White (or cream)—⅝ yd
Blue—⅓ yd
Quilt back—1 yd
Batting—30" x 34"
Binding—⅓ yd
Fusible web—1 yd

Eagles return to our area every year, and scenes like these are commonplace. I've added stars and stripes to this design to create a patriotic wallhanging. Feel free to choose another color combination, substituting your choices for red, white, and blue.

Finished size: 28" x 32"

Cut

Background Fabrics (white or cream)	H—1½" x 14½", cut 2
A—12½" x 12½", cut 1	Outer Border—red, white, and blue
B—6½" x 4½", cut 2	I—1½" x 26½", cut 4 white and 2 red
C—4½" x 6½", cut 1	J—1½" x 22½", cut 4 white and 2 red
D—4½" x 8½", cut 1	K—3½" x 3½", cut 4 blue
E—8½" x 4½", cut 1	Binding
F—4½" x 4½", cut 1	2½" wide strips, cut 4
Inner Border—blue	
G—1½" x 12½", cut 2	

Filler Pieces

Fence units

Use the Speedy Triangle technique:

- Make 13 units 2½" x 4½" (unfinished size).

White—2½" strip, selvage to selvage
Re-cut white into 13 squares, 2½".

Blue—2½" strips, selvage to selvage, cut 2
Re-cut blue into 13 rectangles, 2½" x 4½".

> **Tip:** Make all fences exactly the same so their points are facing the same direction.

Strip-Pieced units

Use the Strip-Pieced Border technique:

- Make these lengths (unfinished sizes):

4½" x 4½"
4½" x 6½"
4½" x 10½", cut 2
Red—1½" strips, selvage to selvage, cut 2
White—1½" strips, selvage to selvage, cut 2

- Make one strata: red + white + red + white. Re-cut into the lengths as listed above.

Construction and Quilting

Refer to the beginning of the chapter for General Construction directions. See Chapter 2, Finishing Your Project, for specific quilting diagrams. This project was quilted with loopty-loops, stipples, a spiky meander, and ¼" inside the fence parts.

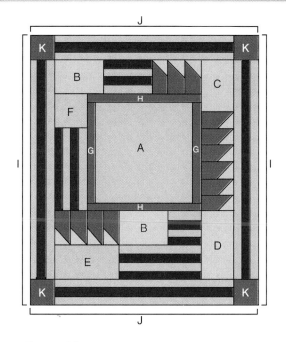

Layout Diagram

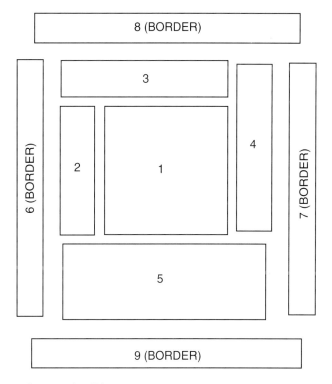

Construction Diagram

Eagles in Flight

By Sally Clouse
of Coeur d'Alene, Idaho, 2002

Yardage Needed

Center block background—fat
  quarter
3 backgrounds—¼ yd
Flying geese and strip units
  Medium—⅓ yd
  Dark—⅓ yd
Inner border—⅛ yd
Outer border—½ yd
Eagles, claw and print, tree—
  ¼ yd
Mountain and water—⅛ yd
Quilt back—1 yd
Batting—30" x 34"
Binding—⅓ yd
Fusible web—1 yd

The layout for this project is Sally's own design. The eagles and claw print are repeated from the Patriotic Eagle project. Sally describes her project: "I decided to do the eagle wallhanging for my son who is an Eagle Scout, and he chose flying geese for the filler pieces. I used a horse fabric for the eagles. To make this work and not have the horses be obvious, I cut the eagle design into smaller pieces, then fused it all back together to form the complete eagle. Not an easy process, but it got the effect I wanted. I machine appliquéd the pieces with nylon thread, outline quilted by machine, and Big Stitched the rest by hand."

Finished size: 28½" x 32½"

Cut

Background Fabrics—cut one each	F—1½" x 12½", cut 2
A—12½" x 12½"	G—1½" x 14½", cut 2
B—6½" x 4½"	
C—4½" x 6½"	Outer Border
D—4½" x 8½"	H—3½" x 26½", cut 2
	I—3½" x 28½", cut 2
Filler Fabric (print fabric)	Binding
E—2½" x 4½", cut 2	2½" wide strips, cut 4
Inner Border	

Filler Pieces

Flying Geese units

Use the Fast Flying Geese technique:

• Make 16, one is excess, 2½" x 4½" (unfinished size).

Medium—2⅞" squares, cut 16
Dark—5¼" squares, cut 4

• Make 16, one is excess, 2½" x 4½" (unfinished size).

Medium—5¼" squares, cut 4
Dark—2⅞" squares, cut 16

Strip-Pieced unit

Use the Strip-Pieced Border technique:

• Make one unit 4½" x 10½" (unfinished size).

Medium—2" x 10½", cut 2
Dark—1½" x 10½"

1. Sew medium + dark + medium.

2. Press seams all one direction.

Construction and Quilting

Refer to the beginning of the chapter for General Construction directions. See Chapter 2, Finishing Your Project, for specific quilting diagrams. Sally combined machine and hand quilting in this project.

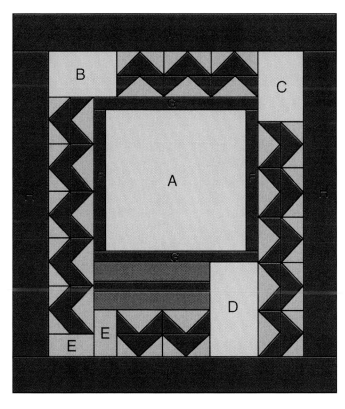

Layout Diagram

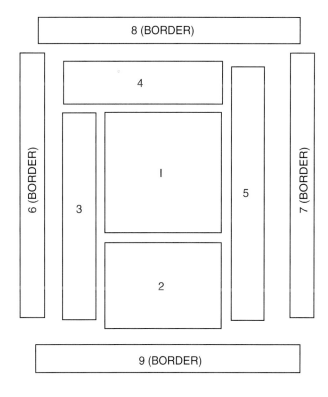

Construction Diagram

Flora and Fauna

by Terrie Kralik, 2002

Look closely at the plants around you as you take your next walk in the forest. You'll probably find some of these flowers and leaves!

Special Note:

The background of the center block is made up of four prints, but it could easily be replaced with one 12½" square. I can imagine this design being embellished with butterflies and bugs, either out of fabric, thread, buttons, or something else three-dimensional. Some of the flowers and plants are a little difficult to cut out. Take your time, be especially careful as you remove the paper backing from them, and handle them as little as possible.

Yardage Needed

Center block background—2 to 4 different ¼ yd pieces or 1 fat quarter

7 backgrounds—⅓ yd

Flying geese and square-in-a-square
  Light—⅓ yd
  Dark—⅓ yd

Inner border—⅛ yd

Outer border
  Medium—½ yd
  Dark—½ yd

Flowers—⅓ yd

Leaves—¼ yd

Quilt back—1 yd

Batting—35" x 32"

Binding—⅓ yd

Fusible web—1 yd

Finished size: 33½" x 30"

Cut

Background Fabrics	Inner Border
A—6½" x 6½", cut 4	G—1½" x 12½", cut 2
B—6½" x 4½", cut 2	H—1½" x 14½", cut 2
C—4½" x 6½", cut 1	Strip-Pieced Outer Border
D—4½" x 10½", cut 1	I—4½" x 22½", cut 2
E—4½" x 8½", cut 2	J—4½" x 34½", cut 2
F—8½" x 4½", cut 1	Binding
	2½" wide strips, cut 4

Filler Pieces

Square-in-a-Square units

Use the Square-in-a-Square technique:

- Make 2 units 4½" square (unfinished size).

Dark—3⅜" squares, cut 2
Light—3" squares, cut 4

Flying Geese units

Use the Fast Flying Geese technique:

- Make 20, 3 are excess, 2½" x 4½" (unfinished size).

Dark—5¼" squares, cut 5
Light—2⅞" squares, cut 20

Outer Strip-Pieced border

Use the Strip-Pieced Border technique:

Verify your exact border measurements before cutting these.

- Make 2 units approx. 4½" wide x 22½"(unfinished size).

- Make 2 units approx. 4½" wide x 34½"(unfinished size).

1. Cut two strips selvage to selvage of approximately eight different fabrics, either dark or medium in value, varying their widths from 1½" to 2". Cut each strip in half, making each approximately 20" long.

2. Arrange these strips in a pleasing order, making three different strata. Sew with ¼" seam and press the seams in one direction.

3. Cut each strata into 4½" segments. Sew them together to make the length needed.

4. Add side borders first, and then add the top and bottom borders.

Construction and Quilting Suggestions

Refer to the beginning of the chapter for General Construction directions. See Chapter 2, Finishing Your Project, for specific quilting diagrams. This project was quilted with a stipple stitch, and in the ditch about every 4" in the outer border.

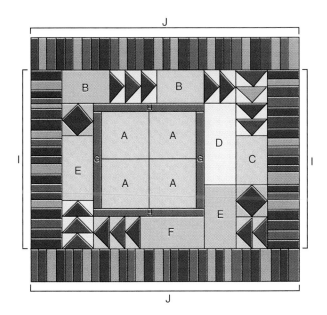

Layout Diagram

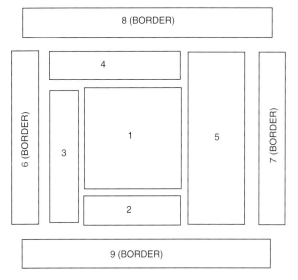

Construction Diagram

Special Note:

The land in the center block couldn't be drawn full-size on one page, so each is shown in two parts in Chapter 5, The Designs. Trace the larger segment onto your fusible web, reposition and connect it with the remaining segment, aligning where it says "connect." Trace the rest of your design. When cutting out these pieces, disregard this inner "connect" line. Cut on the outer edges of the piece as usual.

Yardage Needed

Center block background—fat quarter
5 backgrounds—¼ yd
Checkerboards, strip unit, and square-in-a-square
    Light—¼ yd
    Medium—⅓ yd
    Dark—⅓ yd
Inner border—⅛ yd
Narrow outer border—¼ yd
Wide Strip-Pieced outer border
    Medium—⅝ yd
    Dark—⅝ yd
Birds—¼ yd
Mountains—¼ yd
Greenery—⅛ yd
Quilt back—1¼ yd
Batting—38" x 34"
Binding—⅓ yd
Fusible web—1 yd

Birds of a Feather
by Terrie Kralik, 2002

No forest would be complete without a variety of birds, so I've combined some favorites in this piece. Ducks and geese you've probably seen, but only certain environments will support wild turkeys, quail, or pileated woodpeckers.

Finished size: 36" x 32"

Cut

Background Fabrics—cut one each	
A—12½" x 12½"	H—1½" x 14½", cut 2
B—6½" x 4½"	**Narrow Outer Border**
C—8½" x 4½"	I—1½" x 22½", cut 2
D—5½" x 10½"	J—1½" x 28½", cut 2
E—4½" x 4½"	**Strip-Pieced Outer Border**
F—4½" x 8½"	K—4½" x 24½", cut 2
Inner Border	L—4½" x 36½", cut 2
G—1½" x 12½", cut 2	**Binding**
	2½" wide strips, cut 4

Filler Pieces

Checkerboard units

Use the Checkerboard technique:

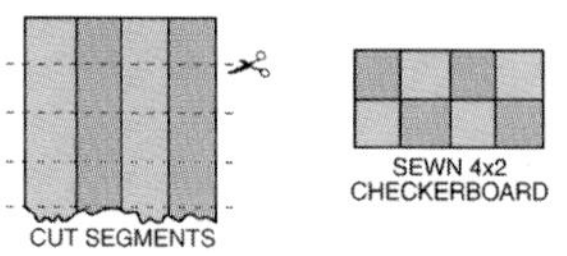

- Make 2 units 4½" x 10½" (unfinished size).

Light—2½" x 27"
Dark—2½" x 27"

1. Re-cut into ten 2½" segments.

2. Sew five segments together to make one unit. Repeat.

Square-in-a-Square

Use the Square-in-a-Square technique:

• Make 7 units 4½" square (unfinished size).

Centers—3⅜" squares, cut 7
Corners—3¼" squares, cut 14

Cut the 3¼" squares on the diagonal once to form triangles.

Strip-Pieced unit

Use the Strip-Pieced Border technique:

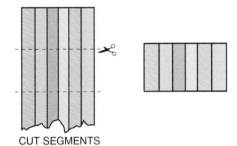

CUT SEGMENTS

• Make 1 unit 3½" x 10½" (unfinished size).

From each of 5 different fabrics (light, medium, and/or dark)—1½" x 8"

Make 1 strata. Cut it into 3½" segments, sew the segments together, and trim it to the correct length.

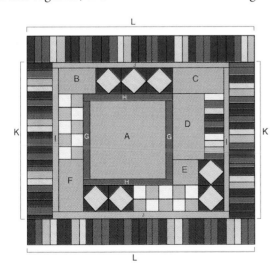

Layout Diagram

Outer Strip-Pieced Border

Use the Strip-Pieced Border technique:

ASSEMBLED STRIP-PIECED BORDER

Verify your exact border measurements before cutting these.

• Make 2 units approximately 4½" x 24½".

• Make 2 units approximately 4½" x 36½".

1. Cut a total of 8 to 12 strips of light, medium, and dark fabrics, cutting 1½" to 2½" wide and selvage to selvage. *Note: Accent color strips should be cut 1½" wide so as not to overpower the border.*

2. Cut each strip in half, making each approximately 20" long. Arrange them in a pleasing order, and sew three different strata.

3. Cut the strata into 4½" segments. Sew them together to make the length needed.

4. Add the side borders first, and then add the top and bottom borders.

Construction and Quilting

Refer to the beginning of the chapter for General Construction directions. See Chapter 2, Finishing Your Project, for specific quilting diagrams. In addition to the usual quilting, I added flowers inside the square-in-a-square pieces, a strand of leaves in both narrow borders, and large loops or "Ls" in the outer border.

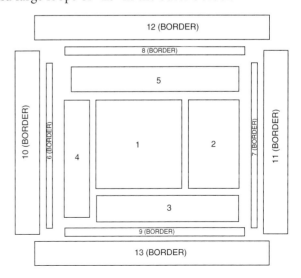

Construction Diagram

Checkerboard Elk

Designed by Sandy Kralik, age 14
Sewn and quilted by Terrie Kralik, 2002

■ I asked my teenage daughter to choose elements from my other projects to include in her own original design, and then to
■ select fabrics. She came up with the layout of the filler pieces (after some simplification by me), and the result is this fun design.
■ I'm surprised at how effective it is with the bright and bold prints!

Special Note:

The filler units and border are unique to this project, but all design elements are borrowed from other projects. From Disappearing Moose: all trees, the land piece in the center block, and the moose tracks. From Tread Lightly: flower (cut 2). From Bear Collage: Bear paw print and leaf (cut 2). From Majestic Elk: elk.

When deciding on fabrics for the checkerboard units in this project, I sewed up three different fabric combinations. I laid these pieces out on my design wall and chose my favorites and their placement. I think it adds interest by having such a variety of fabrics, even though the value of colors is the same. Finally, notice how busy the background fabrics are compared to the other projects.

■ ■ ■

Yardage Needed

Center block background—fat quarter
6 backgrounds—⅓ yd
Checkerboards, square-in-a-square, half-square triangles, filler rectangles
     Medium—½ yd
     Dark—½ yd
Inner border—⅛ yd
Narrow outer border—¼ yd
Wide outer border—½ yd
Elk, trees, bear paw—¼ yd
Leaves, elk tracks—⅛ yd
Quilt back—1 yd
Batting—33" x 36"
Binding—⅓ yd
Fusible web—1 yd

Finished size: 31" x 34½"

Cut

Background Fabrics	J—1½" x 14½", cut 2
A—12½" x 12½"	
B—4½" x 4½"	Narrow Outer Border
C—6½" x 4½"	K—1½" x 26½", cut 2
D—4½" x 10½"	L—1½" x 24½", cut 2
E—8½" x 4½"	
F—10½" x 5½"	Wide Outer Border
G—4½" x 8½"	M—3½" x 28½", cut 2
	N—3½" x 30½", cut 2
Filler Fabric (print)	
H—2½" x 3½", cut 2	Binding
Inner Border	2½" wide strips, cut 4
I—1½" x 12½", cut 2	

Filler Pieces

Half-Square Triangle units

Use the Half-Square Triangle technique:

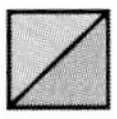

• Make 8 units 2" (unfinished size).

Light—2⅛" squares, cut 4
Dark—2⅜" square, cut 4

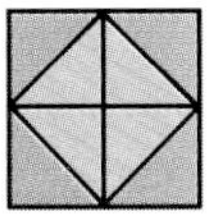

• Make 8 units 2½" (unfinished size).

Light—2⅞" squares, cut 4
Dark—2⅞" square, cut 4

Sew together to look like a square-in-a-square. Make 2.

Checkerboard units

Use the Checkerboard technique:

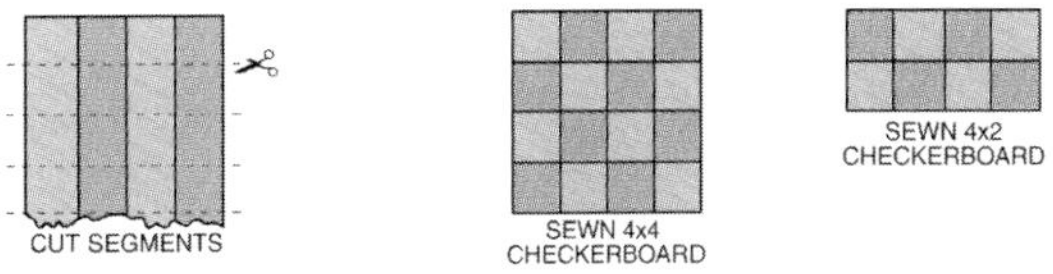

CUT SEGMENTS   SEWN 4x4 CHECKERBOARD   SEWN 4x2 CHECKERBOARD

4 squares x 6 squares—(unfinished size 4½" x 6½"), make 2
4 squares x 8 squares—(unfinished size 4½" x 8½"), make 1
4 squares x 4 squares—(unfinished size 4½" x 4½"), make 2
2 squares x 4 squares—(unfinished size 2½" x 4½"), make 1

Light—1½" strips, selvage to selvage, cut 4
Dark—1½" strips, selvage to selvage, cut 4

1. Cut strips in half to make a length of approximately 20". *Note: Three 20" strips of both dark and light yields a unit of about 4 squares x 10 squares.*

2. Make a four-strip strata—light + dark + light + dark. Press seams all one direction. Cut the strata into segments measuring 1½" wide.

3. Rearrange the pieces to form checkerboards of the sizes given. Repeat, making pairs of light and dark strips until you have made all the checkerboard units needed.

> **Tip:** Lay out the fabrics on a design board in smaller pieces to see if you like the color combination or need more of a certain color.

Construction and Quilting

Refer to the beginning of the chapter for General Construction directions. See Chapter 2, Finishing Your Project, for specific quilting diagrams. I quilted most of this with a stipple, and stitched diagonal lines in the checkerboards. Anything more complex would have been lost in the busy fabrics.

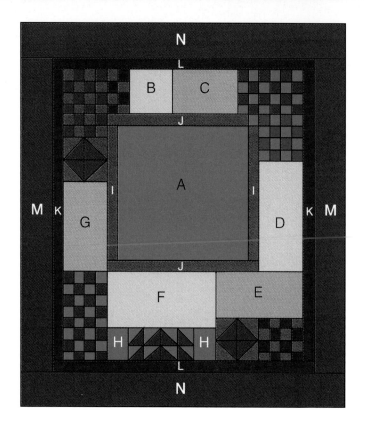

Layout Diagram

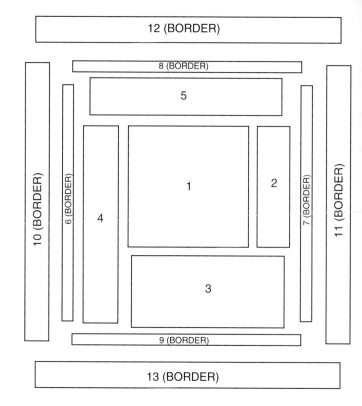

Construction Diagram

CHAPTER 4
Other Projects

Two Square Quilt

By Terrie Kralik, 2002
Quilted by Dawn Kelly of Sagle, Idaho

Special Note:

You will see that I've listed yardage and cutting amounts for borders both "cut cross grain" and "cut along length." By cutting your borders along the length, or on the straight of grain (parallel with the selvage), you will add strength and stability to the quilt because the woven fabric is strongest in this direction. It requires more fabric, so quilters will often piece the border length from pieces cut "cross grain." Choose the yardage for your favorite way of cutting the borders.

This fast and easy quilt makes the most of a novelty print and two accompanying fabrics. Fussy cut the center squares to select the best parts of your print, and put it all together with simple piecing.

Teachers!

Look in Chapter 2, For Teachers Only, to find a class outline and newsletter description for this particular project. It's a great class for all skill levels.

Tip: If you have chosen a large novelty print that has lots of empty space between "good pieces," get extra yardage to allow flexibility with fussy cutting.

Finished size: 49" x 65"

Yardage Needed

40" usable width assumed

	Nine Patch	Lap	Twin	Queen
Approx. finished size				
without border	27" x 27"	43" x 59"	75" x 91"	91" x 107"
with border	34" x 34"	51" x 67"	83" x 99"	99" x 115"
# of blocks	9	35	99	143
Block layout	3 x 3	5 x 7	9 x 11	11 x 13
Novelty Print	½ yd	1¼ yd	3 yd	4¼ yd
Contrast #1	⅜ yd	1⅛ yd	2½ yd	3½ yd
Contrast #2	⅜ yd	1⅛ yd	2½ yd	3½ yd
Border				
Cut cross grain or	½ yd	1 yd	1¼ yd	1¾ yd
Cut along length	1 yd	2 yd	3 yd	3½ yd
Quilt back	1 yd	3 yd	6 yd	9¾ yd
Batting	36" x 36"	53" x 69"	86" x 102"	105" x 113"
Binding	⅓ yd	½ yd	¾ yd	1 yd

	Nine Patch	Lap	Twin	Queen
Novelty print				
—6" squares	9	35	99	143
Contrast #1				
—1¾" strips	6	19	46	65
Contrast #2				
—1¾" strips	6	19	46	65
Border				
—(cut width)	4" wide	4½" wide	4½" wide	4½" wide
Cut cross grain or	4	6	9	11
Cut along length	4	4	4	4
Binding				
—2 ½" strips				
Cut cross grain	4	6	9	11

❄ After sewing Contrast #1 and Contrast #2 strips together (see Construction), cut these segments:

	Nine Patch	Lap	Twin	Queen
6" segments	24	82	218	310
1¾" segments	32	96	240	336

❄ Make this number of checkerboards for your project, using the 1¾" segments:

	Nine Patch	Lap	Twin	Queen
Four Patches	16	48	120	168

Before cutting other pieces, cut your borders and set them aside until later in the project.

Construction

1. Fussy cut the required number of 6" squares from your novelty print. Keep in mind the grain of the fabric, and try to cut these on the straight or cross grain, rather than on the bias. (If you must cut on the bias, take extra care as you sew, to keep distortion to a minimum.)

2. Pair up each strip of Contrast #1 with a strip of Contrast #2. Place RST and sew along the length with an accurate ¼" seam. Repeat with the remaining strips. Press to the darker fabric. The width of these new strips should be 3". Verify and make corrections to each as needed by taking wider or narrower seams. Press well.

❄ A. Refer to the chart, and cut the number of 6" segments as listed for your size project.

❄ B. Refer to the chart and cut the number of 1¾" segments as listed for your size project. Place two segments together, forming a Four Patch or Checkerboard. The seams will interlock. Sew the number of Four Patch units as listed in the chart for your size project. (See the Checkerboard technique in Chapter 1, Techniques.)

3. Lay the novelty print squares on a design wall, arranging them in a pleasing way and following the layout for your size quilt. For example, the Lap Quilt is five blocks wide and seven blocks tall, so set five squares of your novelty print across and make seven rows of them, leaving space between for the rectangular strip segments and Four Patches.

4. Now place the 6" segments on the design wall. One contrast fabric will surround each novelty square, and then alternate from square to square. For example, Contrast #1 will surround your first square. The second square will be surrounded by Contrast #2, the third square will be surrounded by Contrast #1, and so on. Double check that these are all correct before going on.

5. Add the Four Patches in the empty corners of your design, making sure that the colors alternate with the contrast strips. (It sounds so easy, but take your time and make sure they're right!)

6. Sew each row together, beginning with the top row of Four Patches and strip segments. The second row will be made of strip segments and novelty print squares. To make life simple, press odd rows to the left, even rows to the right.

7. Sew Row 1 to Row 2. Continue adding rows until all rows are connected. Press all rows in one direction,

either up or down—your choice.

8. Measure and add side borders, following the instructions in Chapter 2, Finishing Your Project. Repeat for top and bottom borders.

9. Refer again to Chapter 2, Finishing Your Project, for instructions on layering, quilting, binding, and adding a label to your quilt.

Quilting Suggestions

Curves look great across this geometric design, so consider quilting with curves. The outer border is wide enough to add a fancy design, and my quilter added a floral design with loops.

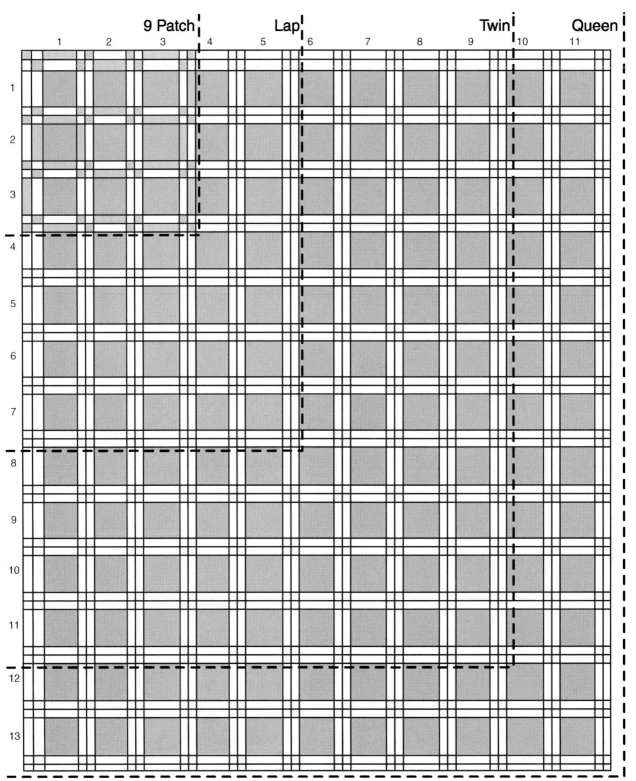

Layout Diagram

Nine Patch Design Variations

These Nine Patch designs began the same as the larger quilt, but each developed its own personality. The sample in blues with birds is great without borders, since one of the contrast fabrics has such movement. No fabric I auditioned with this piece looked right, so I omitted the border altogether.

The Nine Patch made with the duck print looked more interesting with a border, and even better after exchanging some Four Patch units for 3" squares of the border fabric. After fussy cutting some ducks from the fabric, I hand appliquéd them onto the lower edge of the border, adding another personal touch.

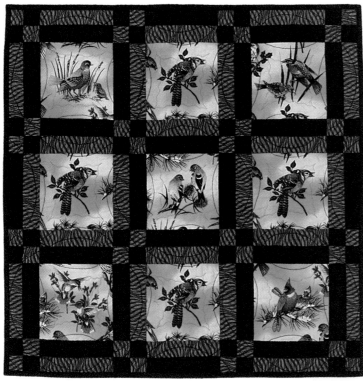

By Terrie Kralik, 2002

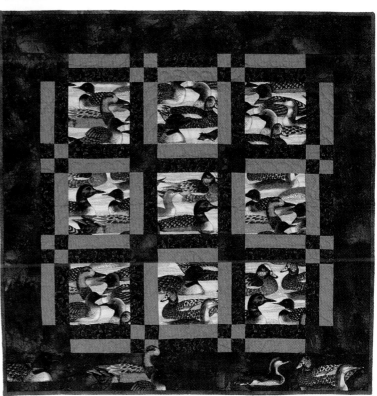

By Terrie Kralik, 2002

Two Square Pillowcase

By Terrie Kralik, 2002

Isn't it fun when you have a quilt and coordinated accessories? Here's a pillowcase that matches the Two Square Quilt, made with only six blocks. Sweet dreams!

Finished size: 21" x 31½"

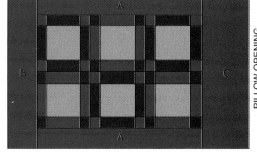

Yardage Needed

Novelty print—¼ yd
Contrast #1—⅛ yd
Contrast #2—⅛ yd
Borders and pillowcase back—
   1⅛ yd

Cut

Novelty Print 6" squares, cut 6	From this, cut five 1¾" x 6" pieces and two 1¾" squares
Contrast #1 1¾" wide strip, cut 2 From this, cut five 1¾" x 6" pieces and two 1¾" squares	Borders A—3" x 24½", cut 2 B—4½" x 21½" C—7½" x 21½"
Contrast #2 1¾" wide strip, cut 2	Pillowcase Back 21½" x 35½"

Construction

1. With the remaining strips of Contrast #1 and Contrast #2, follow Step 2 of the Construction directions for the Two Square Quilt. Cut seven 6" segments and ten 1¾" segments. Make two Four Patches using four of the 1¾" segments.

2. Follow the Pillowcase Layout Diagram to layout the complete top. Sew the top together, as in Steps 6 and 7 of the Two Square Quilt. Add border A, B, and then C. Note that the pillowcase will open at Border C. If you prefer it to open on the other side, reverse pieces B and C.

3. Place the pillowcase top RST with the back. Pin on three sides, leaving it open along Border C. Sew with a ¼" seam, backstitching at the beginning and end of stitching.

4. Fold the raw edge of the pillowcase opening under ¼". Press. Stitch near the raw edge, securing the folded edge. For this stitching, use a longer stitch length than normally used for piecing. Fold under again, this time 3" from the folded edge. Top stitch near the folded edge, through all three layers, backstitching at the beginning and the end. I suggest that you look at the pillowcases on your bed, and this will all make perfect sense.

5. Finish the raw edges of your seams if desired. This can be done with a serger, or use a zigzag stitch on your regular sewing machine. Turn RSO and enjoy! (Remember to set your stitch length back to your normal length.)

Layout Diagram

Two Square Throw Pillow

By Terrie Kralik, 2002

Another fun accessory for your couch or bed is this throw pillow. You may even have enough material left over from your Two Square Quilt to make this!

Finished size: 16" square

Yardage Needed

Novelty print—¼ yd
Contrast #1—⅛ yd
Contrast #2—⅛ yd
Pillow back—fat quarter
16" pillow form

Cut

Novelty Print	Contrast #2
6" squares, cut 4	1¾" wide strip, cut 2
	From this, cut four 1¾" x 6" pieces and two 1¾" squares
Contrast #1	
1¾" wide strip, cut 2	
From this, cut four 1¾" x 6" pieces and two 1¾" squares	Pillow Back
	16½" square

Construction

1. Take the remaining strips of Contrast #1 and Contrast #2. Follow Step 2 of the Construction directions for the Two Square Quilt. Cut four 6" segments and six 1¾" segments. Make one Four Patch from two of the 1¾" segments.

2. Follow the Pillow Layout Diagram to layout the complete pillow. Sew the top together, as in Steps 6 and 7 of the Two Square Quilt.

3. Place the pillow top RST with the pillow back. Stitch around all sides, leaving a 9" opening along the bottom edge. Sew with a little larger than ¼" seam. Stay stitch over the pillow top seams in this opening to prevent the seams from ripping apart when you insert the pillow form.

4. Turn RSO. Press.

5. Gently stuff the pillow form into the pillow. If needed, add loose stuffing in the pillow corners to fill them out.

6. Hand stitch the opening closed, using a blind stitch.

Layout Diagram

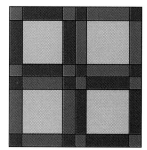

Rows in the Forest

By Terrie Kralik, 2002
Quilted by Dawn Kelly of Sagle, Idaho

I had always wanted to make a row quilt, but never had the time to make one when my friends organized an exchange. I'm sure I'm not the only one in this situation, so my answer is this project: a row quilt you make for yourself! No need to pass it between friends unless you want to, and you can set your own timeline.

Finished size: 68" x 94"

Yardage Needed

Row 1, Mountains
Light—¼ yd
Medium—¼ yd
Dark—½ yd

Row 2, Tall Pines
Background—¾ yd
Green—½ yd
Brown—⅛ yd

Row 3, Square-in-a-Square
Novelty prints (total)—½ yd
Backgrounds (total)—½ yd

Row 4, Moose & Trees
Background—¾ yd
Moose—⅓ yd
Trees—¼ yd

Row 5, Two Square
Novelty Print—⅜ yd
Dark Contrast—¼ yd
Medium Contrast—¼ yd

Row 6, Pickle Jars
Background—⅓ yd
Novelty Print—⅓ yd
Jar Lid—⅛ yd

Row 7, Layered Trees
Background—⅔ yd
Green—⅔ yd

Row 8, Diamonds
Light—¼ yd
Dark—¼ yd

Row 9, Zig Zag
Light—⅓ yd
Dark—⅓ yd

2" strips between rows
1¾ yds cut along the length (or pieced from ⅛ yd each)
4½" borders
Cut cross grain—1⅛ yd or
Cut along length—2¾ yd

Fusible web—1 yd
Back—6 yd
Batting—72" x 98"
Binding—1 yd

Row 1, Mountains

Use the Mountains (Half an Hourglass) technique:

- Make 20 units, one is excess, 6½" square (unfinished size).
Light—7¼" squares, cut 5
Medium—7 ¼" squares, cut 5
Medium (filler pieces)—4" x 6½", cut 2
Dark—6⅞" squares, cut 10
Upper row—1 filler piece, 9 mountain blocks, and 1 filler piece
Lower row—10 mountain blocks

1. Sew the light plus medium squares first, making half-square triangles. Trim to 6⅞" square.

2. Add dark squares to the half-square triangles, as instructed in the Mountains technique.

3. Arrange the mountains as desired. Sew them together, forming two rows, as listed above. You will have one mountain unit left over.

4. Sew the two rows together, matching centers. Trim the excess off the filler pieces. The row length should be 60½" unfinished.

Row 2, Tall Pines

- Make 12 "Old Growth" 4½" x 8½" (unfinished size, including trunk).
- Make 3 "Young Growth" 4½" x 8½" (unfinished size, including trunk).

Trunk

Use the Strip-Pieced Border technique:

Background (abbreviated Bk)

2" strips, cut 2

1¼" x 20" strips, cut 2

Trunk (abbreviated T)

1½" strip

2" x 20" strip

1. Make one strata: 2" Bk + 1½" T + 2" Bk. The strata width should be 4½". Press to the trunk.

2. Cut six 2½" segments and three 4½" segments.

3. Make one strata: 1¼" Bk + 2" T + 1¼" Bk. The strata width should be 4½". Press to the trunk.

4. Cut six 2½" segments.

Tree

Use the Tall Pines technique:

Old Growth

Green—4½" x 6¾", cut 12

Background—3" x 8", cut 12

Young Growth

Green—4 ½" (width) x 4 ¾", cut 3

Background—3" x 6", cut 4

1. Follow the process listed in the Tall Pines technique to make the trees.

2. Place a tree together with its trunk, making trees that measure 8½" tall unfinished. Sew. Press seams open.

3. Arrange 15 trees as desired, and sew them into a row. Press the seams open. The row length should be 60½" unfinished.

Row 3, Square-in-a-Square

Use the Square-in-a-Square technique:

• Make 8 approximately 8¼" square (unfinished size).

Novelty print—6" squares, cut 8

Backgrounds—4⅞" square, cut 2 per block for a total of 16; cut each square once on the diagonal

1. Press seams to the background fabrics.

2. Arrange the blocks in a pleasing order. Sew, matching points where inner squares touch. *Tip: Baste across this point, check for accuracy, and then sew.*

3. The row length should be approximately 66½" unfinished. Mark the center of the row. Equal amounts will be trimmed from the outer two blocks.

Row 4, Moose and Trees

Follow instructions in Chapter 1, Using Fusible Web.

Background—10½" x 10½", cut 6

Moose (from Disappearing Moose wallhanging project), cut 4

Large tree (unique to this project, found in Chapter 5, The Designs), cut 5

1. Arrange the backgrounds in a pleasing order. Sew them together to make a row. Position the moose and trees, fuse in place.

2. Machine appliqué the raw edges, if desired, using a tight zigzag stitch. Row length should be 60½" unfinished.

Row 5, Two Square

Use the Strip Pieced Border technique:

Novelty print—6" squares, cut 7

Dark contrast

1¾" wide strips, cut 3

2¼" x 22"

Re-cut one 1¾" wide strip into eight 1¾" x 6" rectangles

Medium contrast

1¾" wide strips, cut 3

2¼" x 22"

Re-cut one 1¾" wide strip into six 1¾" x 6" rectangles

1¾" wide strips

1. Sew one dark + one medium RST along length. Press to the dark. Repeat for the other pair of strips.

2. From these, cut six 6" segments and twelve 1¾" segments.

2¼" wide strips

Sew one dark strip + one medium strip RST along the length. Press to the dark. From this strata, cut two 6" segments and four 1¾" segments. These are called WIDE segments.

Row Construction

1. Refer to the photo for general layout information. Arrange your novelty squares in a pleasing order, leaving space between them. Place a dark rectangle above and below the first novelty square; place a medium rectangle above and below the second novelty square. Repeat for the rest of the row.

2. Add the 6" segments between novelty prints. The left-most square will be surrounded by your dark contrast fabric; the next novelty square will be surrounded by your medium contrast, etc.

3. Add the Wide 6" segments and Wide 1¾" segments to each end of your design.

4. Sew the Two Square rows:

Row 1: Wide 1¾" segment + Dark rectangle + 1¾" segment + Medium rectangle + 1¾" segment, etc. End with a Wide 1¾" segment.

Row 2: Wide 6" segment + Novelty square + 6" segment + Novelty square + 6" segment, etc. End with a Wide 6" segment.

Row 3: Same as Row 1.

5. Sew the rows together, pressing towards the contrast fabrics.

6. Trim the row length to 60½" unfinished.

Row 6, Pickle Jars

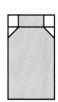

• Make 12 units 4½" x 7" (unfinished size).
Novelty print—4½" x 6", cut 12

Jar Lid—2½" x 20", cut 1

Background

2½" x 7"

1½" strips, cut 4

From the 1½" background strips, cut:

1½" x 7", cut 11 (spacer strips)

1½" x 20", cut 2

1½" squares, cut 24

Jar Lid Unit

Use the Strip-Pieced Border technique:

1. Sew this strata: 20" strip background + 20" strip jar lid + 20" strip background. Press seams to the jar lid. Strata should measure 4½" wide.

2. Cut this strata into twelve 1½" segments.

Jar

Use the Speedy Triangle technique:

Tip: Make a template to audition your novelty prints. Cut a 4½" x 6" rectangle of paper or cardboard. Mark ¼" seams and corner triangle pieces. Cut out the center. Take it with you when you are choosing your jar contents!

1. Add 1½" squares to the upper corners of the novelty print rectangles. Press to the background. Use an "Add-a-Quarter" ruler to trim off the excess.

2. Sew a jar lid unit to each jar. Press to the lid.

3. Arrange the jars in a pleasing order. Begin with a jar at the edge of the row. Add a 7" long spacer strip between jars, placing the wider strip wherever you'd like. Sew the row together. Press the seams to the spacer strips. Row length should be 60½" unfinished.

Row 7, Layered Trees

Use the Speedy Triangle technique:

• Make 12 units 5½" x 8½" (unfinished size).

Green

    3" x 5½", cut 9

    2½" x 5½", cut 30

    2" x 5½", cut 9

Background

    3½" square, cut 10

    3" square, cut 8

    2½" square, cut 18

    2" square, cut 60

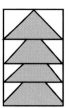

• Make 4	Green	Background
	3" x 5½"	3" square
	2½" x 5½"	2½" square
	2" x 5½"	2" square
	2½" x 5½"	2" square

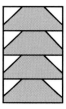

• Make 3	Green	Background
	2½" x 5½"	2" square

(Every layer is the same; make 12 parts.)

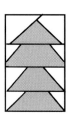

• Make 5	Green	Background
	3" x 5½"	3½" square
	2½" x 5½"	2" square
	2½" x 5½"	2½" square
	2" x 5½"	2" square

1. Sew each green rectangle with its corresponding background squares, using the Speedy Triangle technique. Press to the background. Trim excess fabric, if desired.

2. Sew four tree layers together as in each diagram, making the number of trees needed. Press the seams open, up, or down.

3. Arrange as desired. At this point, you may want to press some trees up and some down where seams align. Or, better yet, rearrange the trees so only a few seams match. The row length should be 60½" unfinished.

Row 8, Diamonds

Use the Half-Square Triangle technique:

• Make 10 units 6½" square (unfinished size).
Dark—4" squares, cut 20
Light—4" squares, cut 20

1. Make 40 half-square triangle units. Trim to 3½" square unfinished.

2. Arrange the units into blocks with four units per block. Refer to the diagram.

3. Sew the blocks together in pairs. Press the seams for the upper half to the right and for the lower half to the left. Sew the two halves together, pressing this seam upward.

4. Sew the blocks together, referring to the photo for color placement. Press the seams open. The row length should be 60½" unfinished.

Row 9, Zig Zag

Use the Half-Square Triangle technique:

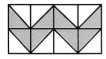

• Make 30 units, 4½" square (unfinished size)
Dark—5" squares, cut 15
Light—5" squares, cut 15

1. Make 30 half-square triangle units. Trim to 4½" square unfinished.

2. Arrange the units in a zigzag pattern, referring to the diagram. Sew in two rows, pressing the seams open.

3. Sew the rows together, pressing the seam open or to one side. The row length should be 60½" unfinished.

Quilt Top Construction

1. Measure the length of each row. Make adjustments so they are all the same. Do this by taking wider or narrower seams. Trim excess off the Square-in-a-Square row and the Two Square row by trimming an equal amount from each end.

2. Cut eight strips 2" x 60½" (or the length of your rows) for spacing strips between rows. Sew the rows and spacing strips together. Press the seams all in one direction.

3. Measure the width of your quilt for the top and bottom borders. Refer to Chapter 2, Finishing Your Project, for details. Cut 4½" wide border strips using your favorite method—either along the length of the fabric (the strongest grain of the fabric) or cut cross grain and piece. Sew on the top and bottom borders. Press the seams to the borders. Measure, cut, and add side borders. Press the seams to the borders.

4. Refer to Chapter 2, Finishing Your Project, for suggestions on layering, quilting, binding, and adding a label to your quilt. You will need nine 2½" wide strips (selvage to selvage) for binding.

Quilting Suggestions

Every row has been quilted differently, based on the block. For example, there are curves quilted into the Square-in-a-Square row; the background of the Moose and Trees row is stippled; a leaf pattern is quilted over each Diamond block; and both the Tall Pines and the Layered Trees rows are quilted to accent the tree shape. Let your imagination go wild, and just have fun quilting your row quilt.

Tablecloth

By Terrie Kralik, 2002

Yardage Needed

(42" usable width assumed)

Light checkerboards—½ yd
Medium checkerboards and
   wide border—1 yd
Dark checkerboards and corner
   stones—¼ yd
Background behind animals—
   ⅔ yd
Animals —¾ yd
Back 48 ½" square—3 yd
Batting (optional)—50" x 50"
Binding (optional)—½ yd
Fusible web—1½ yd

To carry the forest theme from your walls to your table, try this. Choose different animals or add trees or mountains to make it your very own. As shown, use the moose and elk from Disappearing Moose and Majestic Elk and the leaf from Bear Collage. Trace four each.

Finished size: 48" x 48"

Cut

Background	corner stones)
A—10½" x 20½", cut 4	
	Checkerboards
Borders	3" strips, 42" long
B—4½" x 40½", cut 4	Light—cut 4
(medium)	Medium—cut 5
C—4½" x 4½", cut 4 (dark	Dark—cut 1

Use the Checkerboard technique:

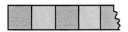

1. Sew one strata with these strips: dark + medium. Press to dark. Cut the strata in half. Sew the halves together, making a strata four strips wide and measuring 10½" in width. If the strata width is not correct, adjust by taking narrower or wider seams. Press seams all one direction. From this strata, cut four 3" segments. These will make up the center portion of the large checkerboard. (Leave as 1 x 4 units.)

2. Sew two strata with these strips: medium + light + medium + light. The strata width should be 10½". Adjust as needed. Cut into twenty-four 3" segments. Arrange the segments into four 4 x 4 checkerboard units, plus eight 1 x 8 checkerboard units. Sew. Press in one direction.

3. Remove the center seam of the remaining strata, forming two units with a medium + light strip each. The strata width should be 5½". From these, cut eight 3" segments.

Construction

1. Follow the layout diagram to arrange the top.

2. Sew the center checkerboard unit. The top and bottom two rows are 1 x 8 checkerboard units of medium + light. Sew the middle rows: (light + medium 1 x 2 unit) + (dark + medium 1 x 4 unit) + (light + medium 1 x 2 unit). Make four middle rows, alternating colors as shown. Sew the rows together, pressing seams all one direction when done.

3. Fuse designs to "A" pieces, as shown in the photo or as you prefer. Refer to Chapter 1, Using Fusible Web, for more information. Pay attention to the direction the animals face, so everyone at the table will have animals right side up. Finish the edges of your designs now, using a machine appliqué stitch (tight zigzag).

4. Sew the tablecloth top together: Top row: 4 x 4 checkerboard unit + "A" + 4 x 4 checkerboard unit. Middle row: "A" + 8 x 8 checkerboard unit + "A." Bottom row: Same as top row. Sew the rows together. Press the seams to the checkerboard throughout.

5. Add "B" border to each side. Press to "B." Sew the border pieces C + B + C. Press the seams to "B." Add the borders to the top and bottom. Press to the borders.

6. Square up the top. Piece the backing as needed to reach the 48½" square size, or the actual measurement of your top. Remember to remove all selvages before sewing. Press the seams open. *Note: Tablecloths don't need batting in them, but often they will have a lightweight filler just for stability. Use flannel, a thin batting, or fleece (interfacing) if you'd like. Rather than detailed and intricate quilting, tack layers together with minimal stitching by hand or machine. If you prefer, bind the tablecloth as you would a quilt.*

7a. Finishing Without Binding: (Pillow-turn method) Place the tablecloth top and back RST, with the back underneath. If using a filler or batting, position the filler below all of this. Sew around the outer edges, leaving a 12" opening. Turn RSO through this opening. Press. Use an invisible stitch to close the opening by hand.

7b. Finish With Binding: Quilt and bind using your favorite method. Refer to Chapter 2 for suggestions on Finishing Your Project.

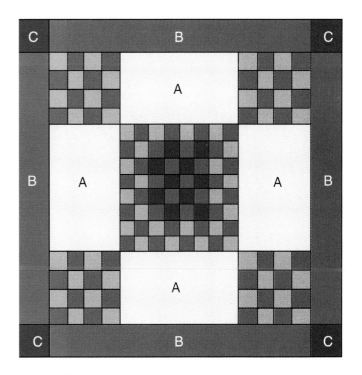

Layout Diagram

Table Runner

By Terrie Kralik, 2002

Yardage Needed
(42" usable width assumed)

Background—⅓ yd
Dark checkerboards and
  border—⅝ yd
Medium checkerboards and
  corner squares—¼ yd
Light checkerboards—¼ yd
Animals—fat quarter
Plants—⅛ yd
Back—1⅜ yd
Batting—22" x 47"
Binding—⅓ yd
Fusible web—1 yd

Here's another project to bring the forest theme into your home. This table runner uses the moose and elk from Disappearing Moose and Majestic Elk; trace one each. The flower and leaf are from Tread Lightly and Flora and Fauna; trace two each.

Finished size: 20" x 45"

Cut

Background	D—2½" x 2½", cut 4
A—10" x 16½", cut 2	medium corner stones
	Checkerboards
Borders	2½" wide strips, approx.
B—2½" x 16½", cut 2 dark	42" long (half strip is 21"
C—2½" x 41½", cut 2 dark	long)
	Dark, cut 3½
	Medium, cut 2
	Light, cut 1½

Use the Checkerboard technique:

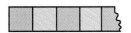

Dark + medium:

1. Make one strata with these full-length strips: dark + medium + dark + medium. Sew with an accurate ¼" seam along the length. Press seams in one direction. The strata width should be 8½".

2. Cut twelve 2½" wide segments.

3. Pair two segments together, sewing along the 2½" side, making a row that is one square tall and eight squares wide. Make sure the colors alternate as in a checkerboard.

4. Repeat to make six rows.

Dark + light:

1. Make one strata with these strips: dark + light + dark (half length) + light (half length). Sew with an accurate ¼" seam along the length. Press seams in one direction. The strata width should be 8½".

2. Cut ten 2½" wide segments. You will probably have to cut and sew one segment from the leftovers of the full-length strips.

3. Pair two segments together, sewing along the 2½" side, making a row that is one square tall and eight squares wide. Make sure the colors alternate as in a checkerboard.

4. Repeat to make five of these rows.

Construction

1. Follow the layout diagram to arrange the checkerboard rows: 3 rows dark + medium; 5 rows dark + light; 3 rows dark + medium.

2. Add "A" pieces with designs already fused to them and edges finished, if desired. Pay attention to the direction the animals face. Press seams to checkerboard.

3. Add "C" border pieces to each side. Press seams to "C".

4. Sew the border pieces D + B +D; press seams to "B." Align the seams and sew one border unit to the top of your table runner. Press to the border. Repeat for the bottom border.

5. Quilt and bind using your favorite method, or refer to Chapter 2 for suggestions on Finishing Your Project.

Layout Diagram

Pillows

By Terrie Kralik, 2002

Pillows at our home are not just for decoration. We really use them! For that reason, I prefer to lightly quilt the pillow top to make it more durable. Choosing heavyweight cotton fabrics also will make it last longer. If you prefer, just make your pillow top and sew it to the back to complete it. I do recommend that you secure the edges of the designs in some way.

Finished size: 14"

Yardage Needed

(for each pillow)

Center background—fat quarter (for Elk, Eagle, or Bear pillow)
—Moose pillow requires ⅓ yd + ⅛ yd

Tuck fabric (for Bear or Moose pillow)—⅛ yd

Dark for animals or plants—¼ yd

Pillow back and borders on front—½ yd

14" pillow form of your choice

Fusible web—½ yd

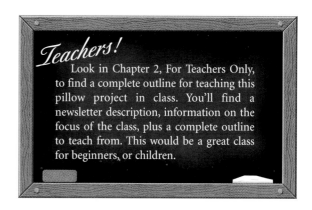

Tips: Each of these pillows could be made into a small wallhanging. Finish the top as you would a quilt, bind the edges, and add a sleeve to hang it.

Another idea is to make your borders asymmetrical. Rather than having them evenly distributed around the center square, try sewing wide borders on the top and left side only.

Tip: If you will be cutting the pillow back and front borders from the same fabric, cut your pillow back first. Cut your borders from the remaining fabric.

General pillow construction

1. Choose your favorite center square design from the wallhangings in Chapter 3, or make your own.

2. Fuse the design in place, following the directions in Chapter 1, Using Fusible Web. Finish the edges of designs as desired.

3. Add borders, as shown in the diagram. If your layout includes tucks, sew the three-dimensional strips of fabric into the seam as you would lace: Cut the pieces as indicated. Fold them in half along the length WST, forming strips ½" wide. Pin the strips to the seam they fit. Lay the border piece of the same length on top of the tuck, sandwiching the tuck between the border piece and the background fabric. Sew as normal, with a ¼" seam. Repeat.

4. Refer to Chapter 2, Finishing Your Project, and Layering & Quilting. Layer the finished pillow top with a piece of batting and a backing fabric. This backing fabric will be inside the pillow, so it can be a fabric you don't like. Make sure the print doesn't show through to the pillow top.

5. Quilt the pillow top, securing the edges of the designs by stitching with a free-motion quilting stitch. Stitch through all layers—the design and background it's fused to, batting, and pillow top backing.

6. Square up the quilted pillow top.

7. Place the pillow top RST with the pillow back. This is the *good* pillow back, the one that will be seen when your pillow is on the couch. Stitch around the pillow using a ¼" seam, leaving an 8" to 10" opening at the bottom. Turn RSO. Press.

8. Insert the pillow form into the pillow through the opening.

9. Hand stitch the opening closed, using your favorite blind stitch.

Pillow 1, Eagle

The center design is from the Patriotic Eagle
wallhanging project in Chapter 3.

Finished sizes: 12" center square with 1" border all
around

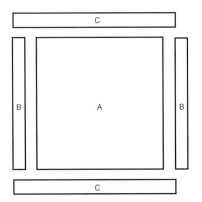

Cut

A—12½" x 12½"
B—1½" x 12½", cut 2
C—1½" x 14½", cut 2

Pillow Back
14½" x 14½"

Pillow 2, Bear and Trees

The bears are from the Bear Collage wallhanging project
in Chapter 3. The trees are unique to this project. You
can find them in Chapter 5, The Designs.

Finished sizes: 12" center square with 1" border all
around and tucks

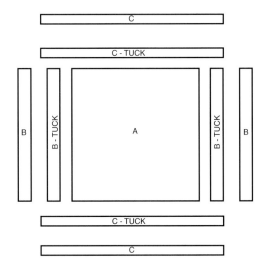

Cut

A—12½" x 12½"
B—1½" x 12½", cut 2
B Tuck—1" x 12½", cut 2
C—1½" x 14½", cut 2
C Tuck—1" x 14½", cut 2

Pillow Back
14½" x 14½"

Pillow 3, Elk

The elk is from the Majestic Elk wallhanging project in Chapter 3.

Finished sizes: 10" center square with 2" border all around

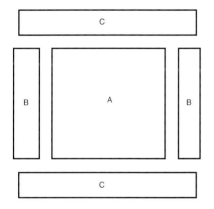

Cut

A—10½" x 10½"
B—2½" x 10½", cut 2
C—2½" x 14½", cut 2

Pillow Back
14½" x 14½"

Pillow 4, Moose and Bear

The moose is from the Disappearing Moose wallhanging project in Chapter 3. The leaves are from the Bear Collage wallhanging project, one facing right, one facing left. The small bears are unique to this project. You can find them in Chapter 5, The Designs.

Rectangular center with two smaller rectangles and tucks

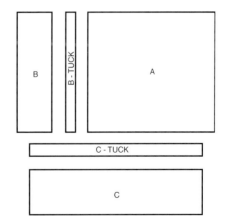

Cut

A—11½" x 10½"
B—3½" x 10½"
B Tuck—1" x 10½"
C—4½" x 14½"
C Tuck—1" x 14½"

Pillow Back
14½" x 14½"

Purchased clothing with designs from Chapter 5, by Terrie Kralik, 2002

The animal designs in Chapter 5 are great to add to purchased clothing, like denim jumpers or vests, chambray shirts, sweatshirts, or aprons. Make a scene or a row of animals, add your favorite embellishments, and have fun wearing a bit of the forest!

Yardage Needed

Animals—fat quarter to ½ yd
Fusible web—½ yd to 1 yd

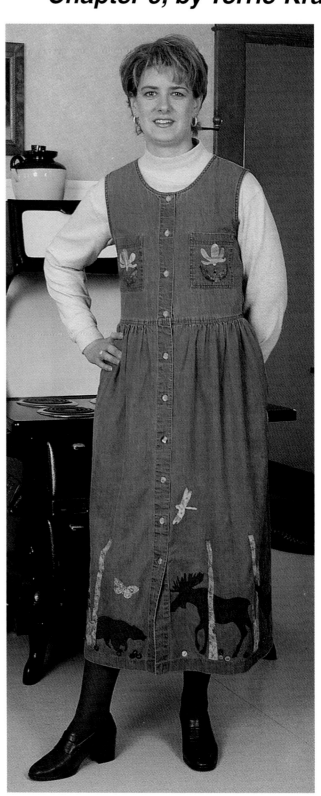

General Construction

1. Follow the directions in Chapter 1, General Instructions for Using Fusible Web. Lay out each animal, tree, and/or plant on your article of clothing. Decide on the placement for everything *before* you fuse anything down.

2. I suggest you finish the edges in some way, both to secure them and to keep them from fraying during laundering.

3. Embellish with buttons, beads, charms, embroidery, silk ribbon work, or paints.

For Sweatshirts

1. Make a panel with the animal design on it. Sew the panel directly to the sweatshirt.

2. Cover the raw edges of the panel with bias tape, turn them under and sew them down by machine, or turn them under and appliqué them by hand.

3. Use the projects and photos for ideas, or make up your own. The size of the panel will depend on the size of the shirt, so experiment to find what you like best.

CHAPTER 5
The Designs

Disappearing Moose

Trace as 1 or 2 separate parts

Connect (land)

Connect

Trace 3

Disappearing Moose

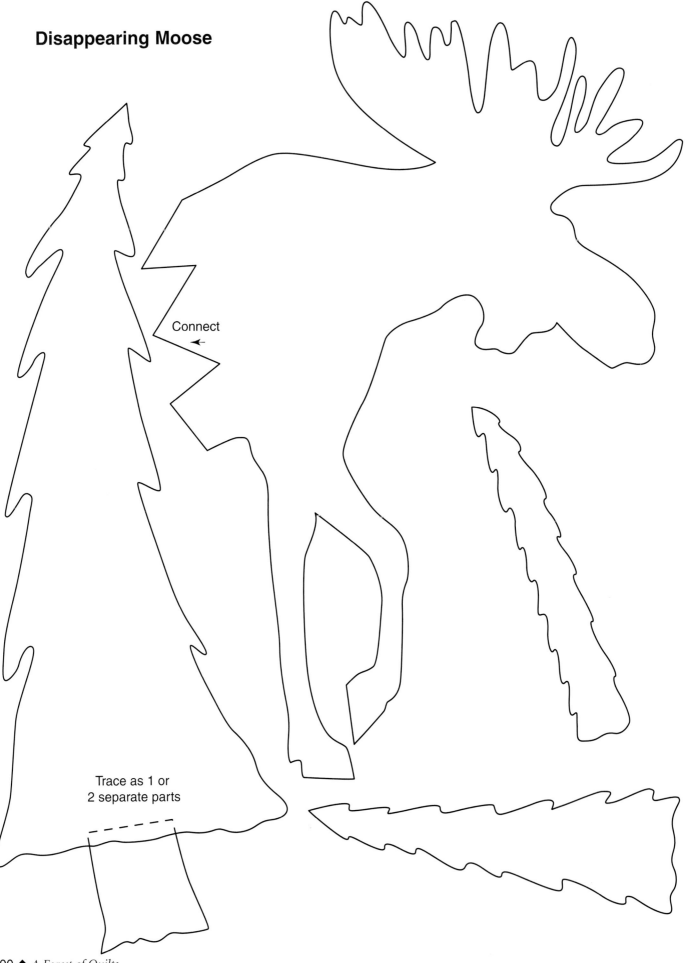

Connect

Trace as 1 or
2 separate parts

Disappearing Moose

Connect (land) →

Water below moose

Trace 2

Tread Lightly

Tread Lightly

Trace as 1
piece or 2

Tread Lightly

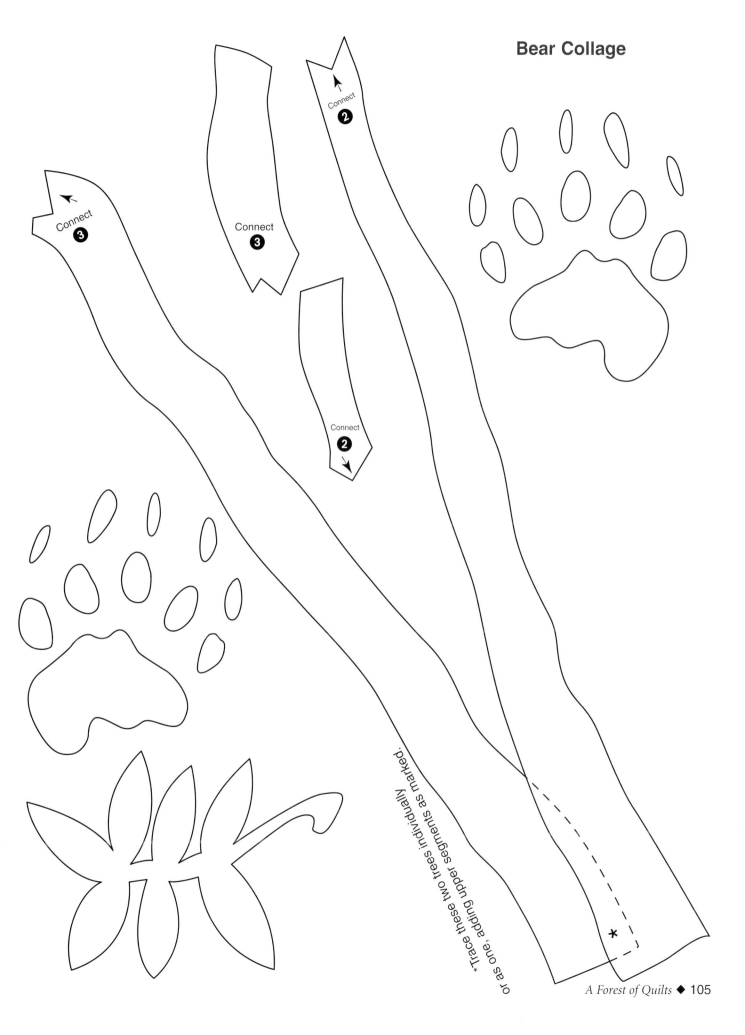

Bear Collage

Connect

2

Connect

3

Connect

3

Connect

2

*Trace these two trees individually
or as one, adding upper segments as marked.

*

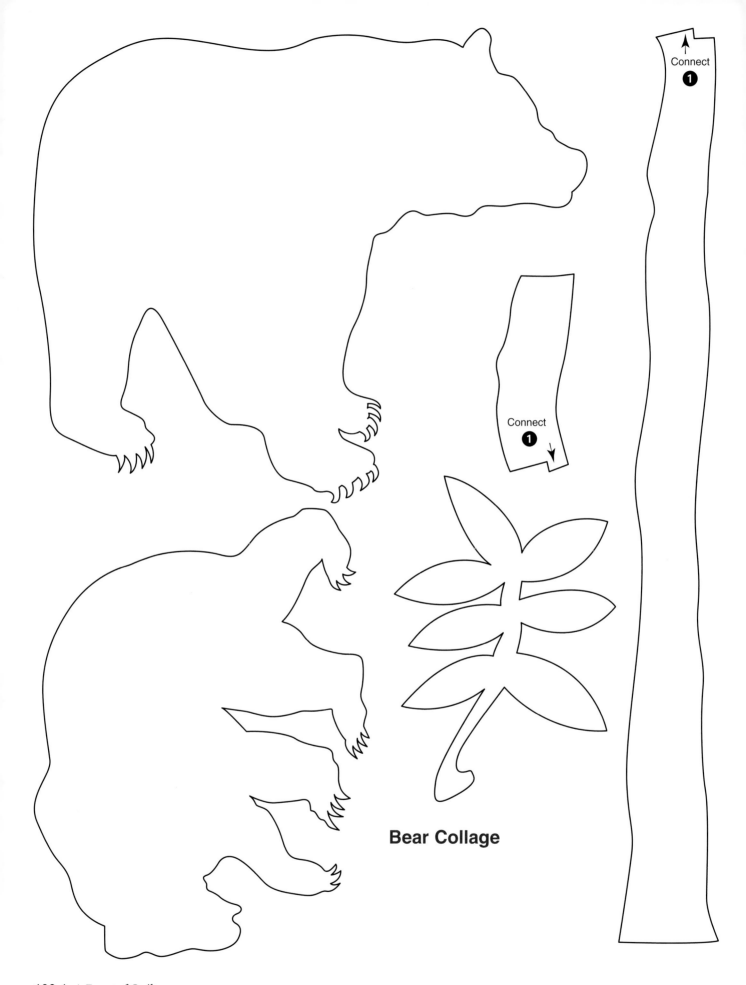

Bear Collage

Connect ❶

Connect ❶

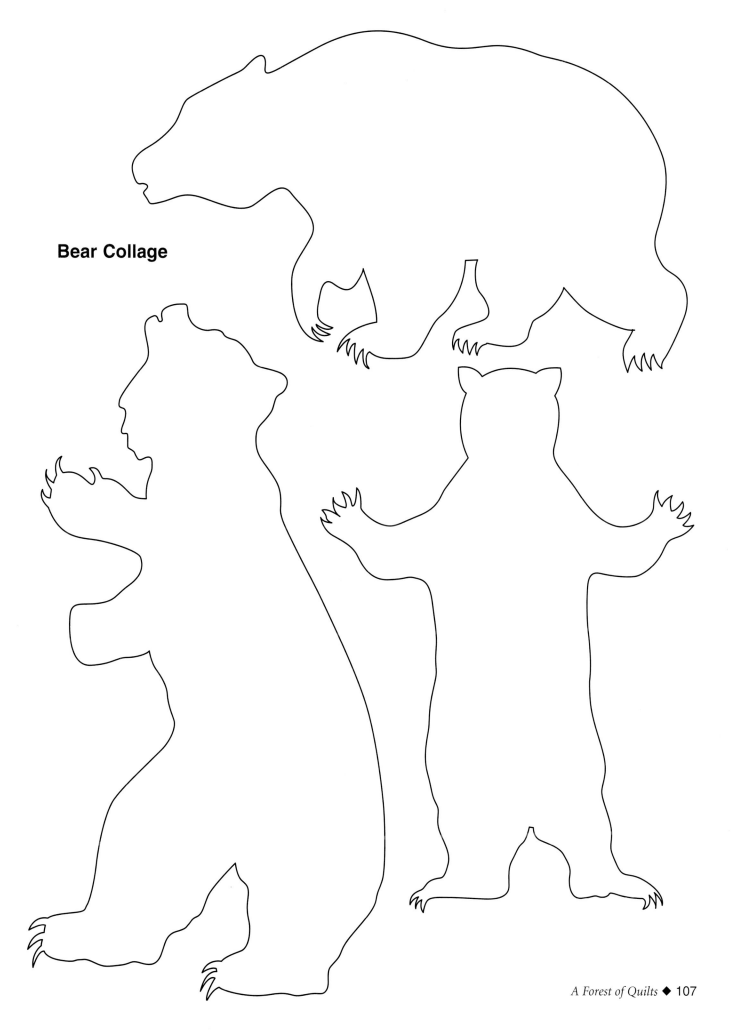

Bear Collage

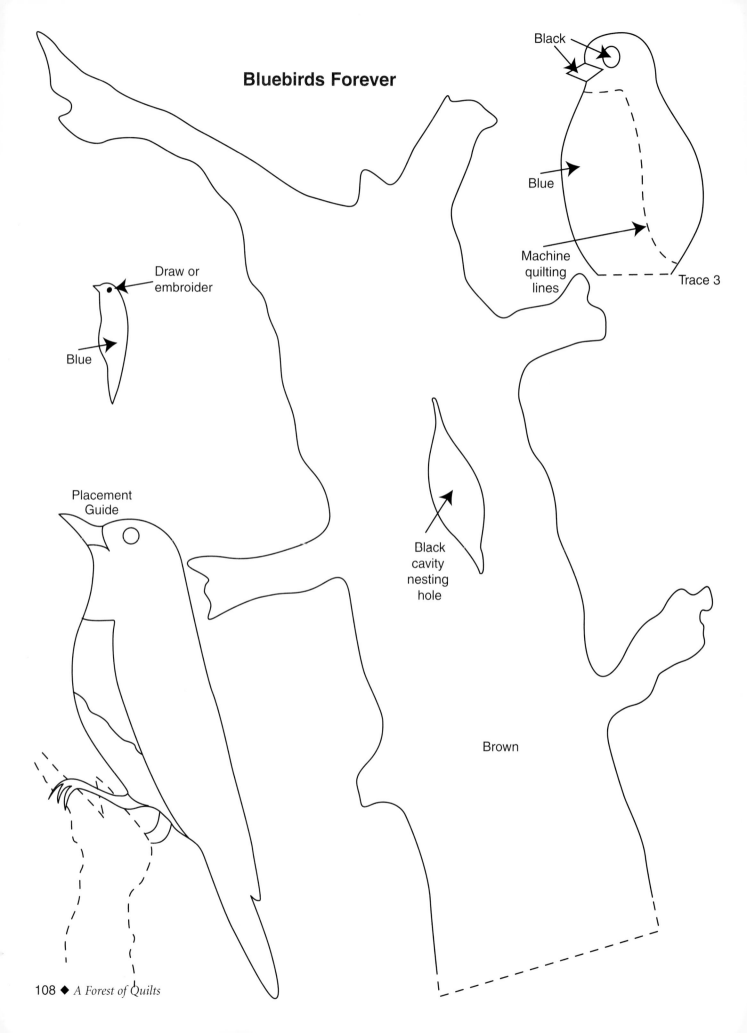

Bluebirds Forever

Black

Blue

Machine
quilting
lines

Trace 3

Draw or
embroider

Blue

Placement
Guide

Black
cavity
nesting
hole

Brown

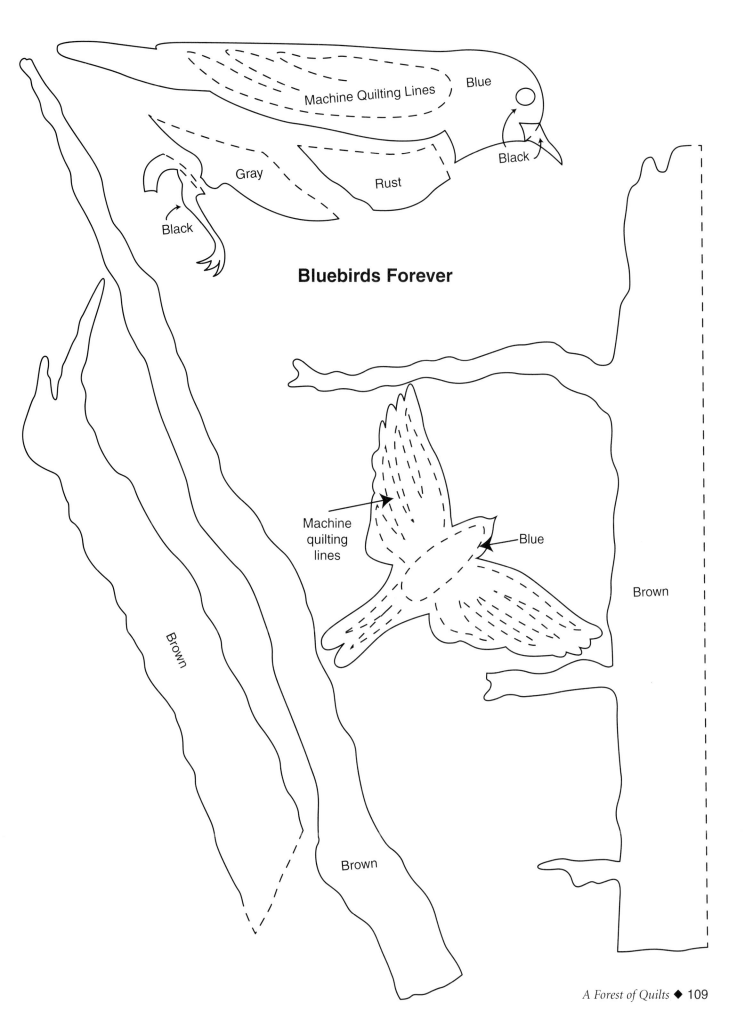

Machine Quilting Lines

Blue

Gray

Rust

Black

Black

Bluebirds Forever

Machine quilting lines

Blue

Brown

Brown

Brown

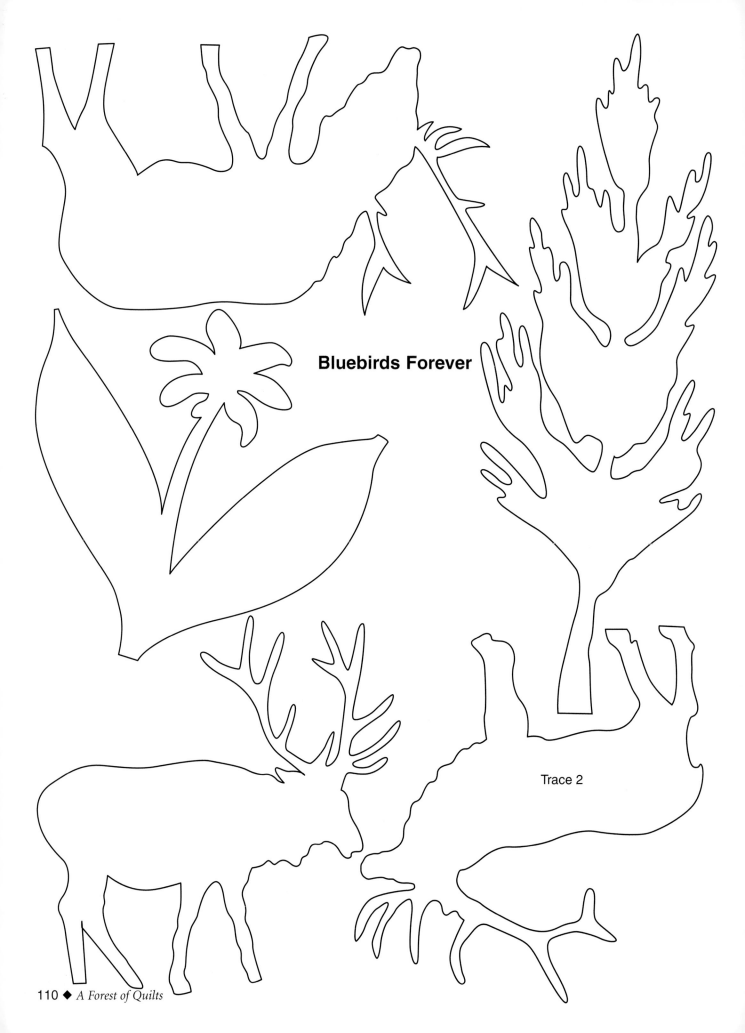

Bluebirds Forever

Trace 2

Majestic Elk

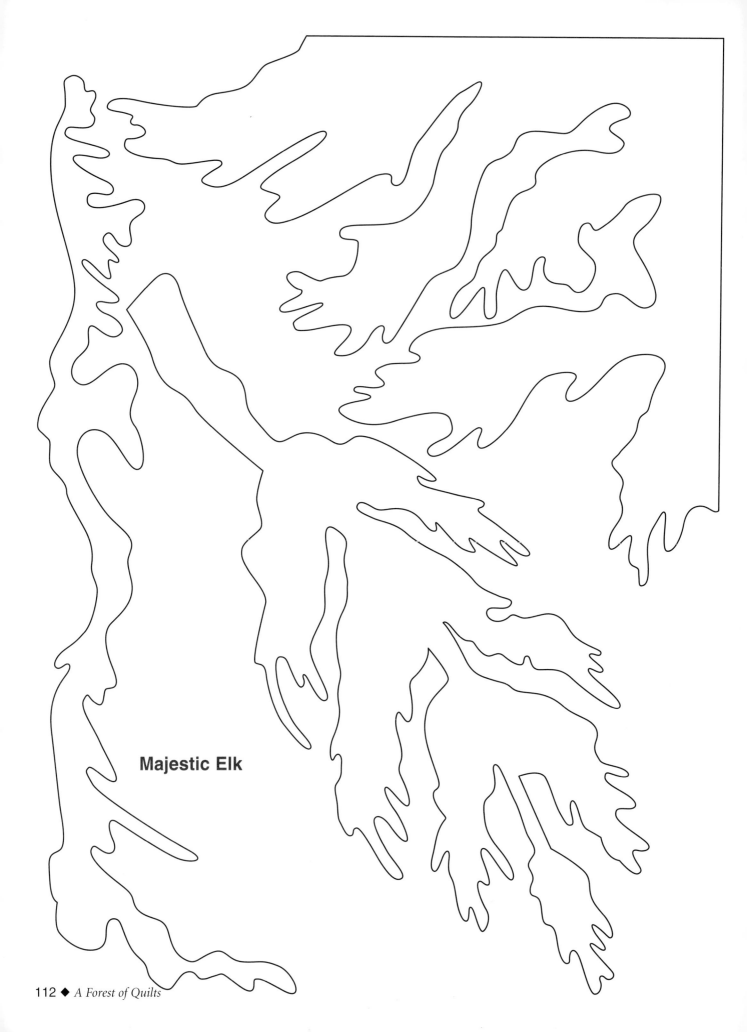

Majestic Elk

Trace 5

Trace 2

Patriotic Eagle

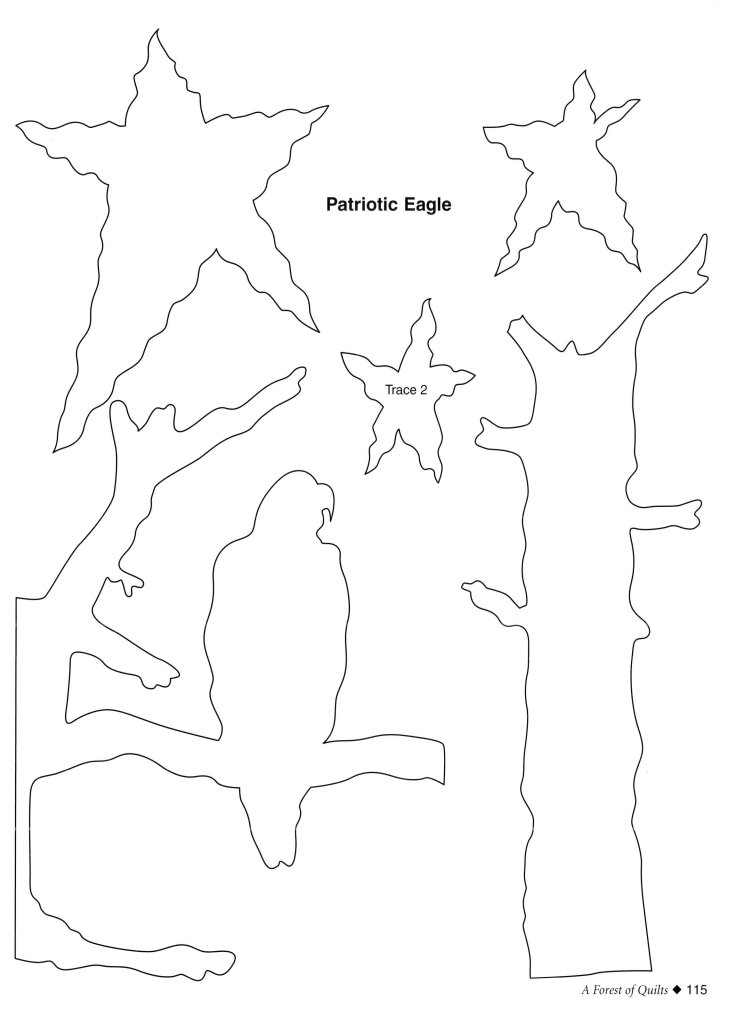

Patriotic Eagle

Trace 2

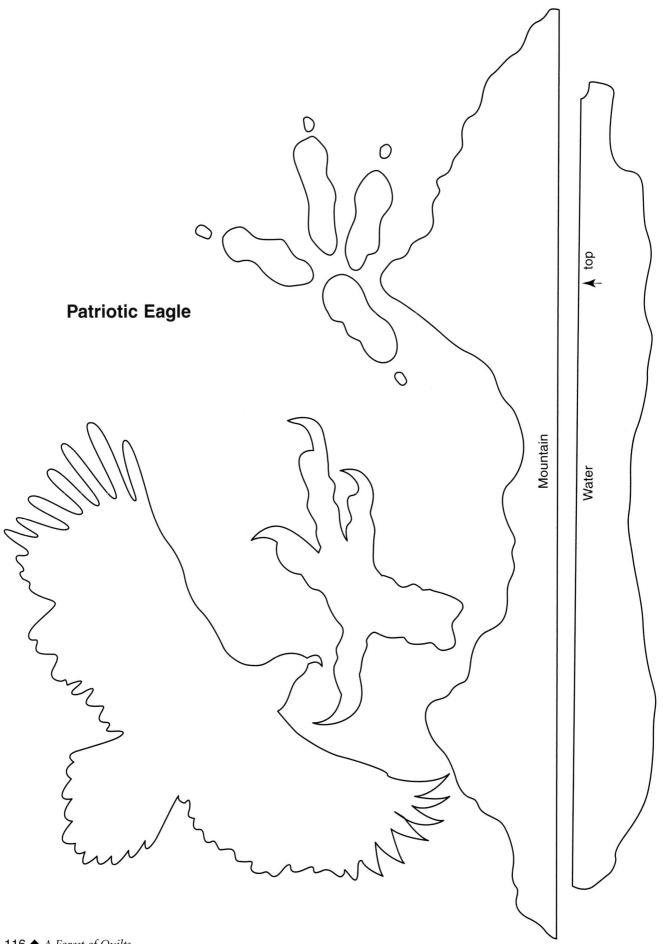

Patriotic Eagle

Mountain

Water

top

Flora and Fauna

Trace 4

Trace 2

Flora and Fauna

Trace 2

Trace 2

Flora and Fauna

Draw or
embroider

Birds of a Feather

Top

Birds of a Feather

Cut Out

Water

Birds of a Feather

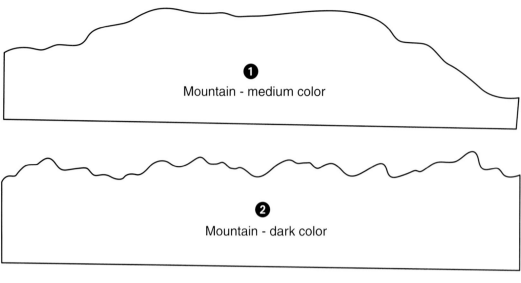

1 Mountain - medium color

2 Mountain - dark color

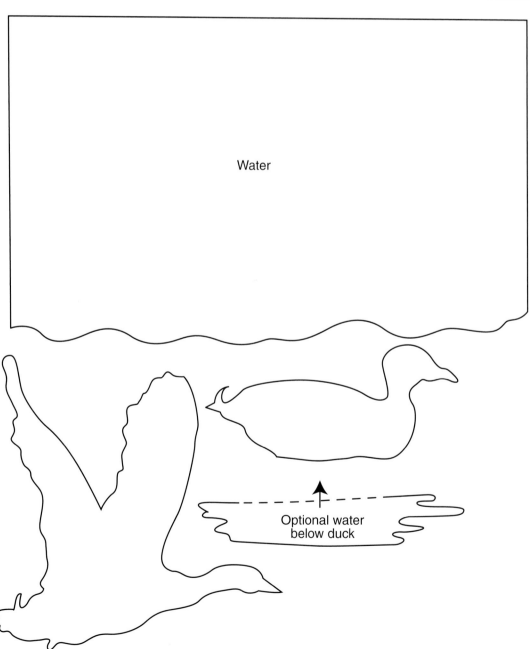

Water

Optional water
below duck

Birds of a Feather

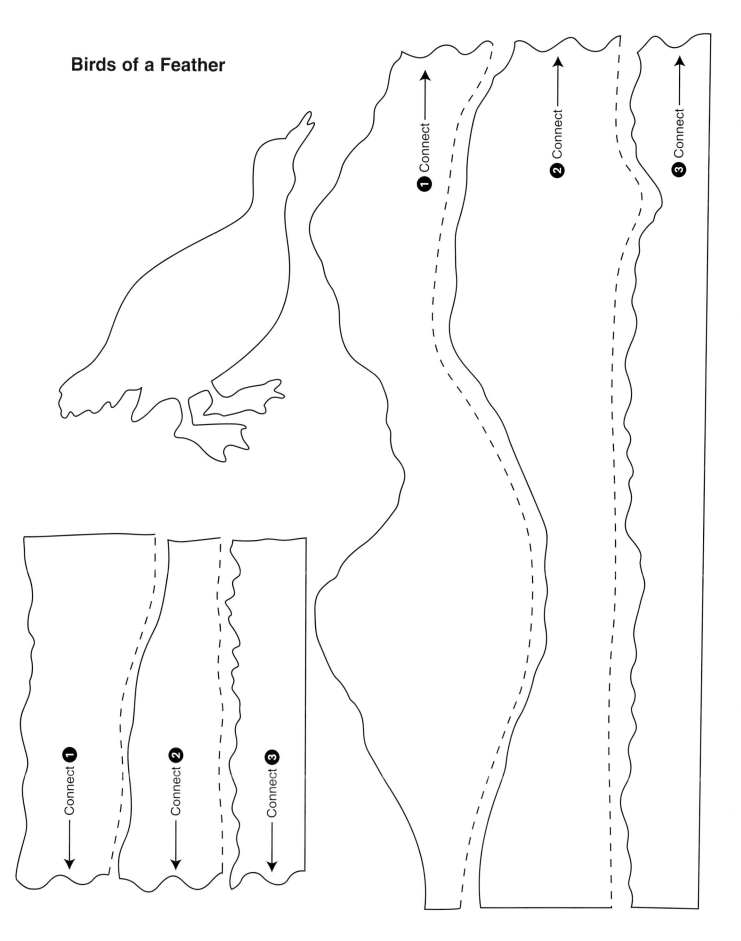

Birds of a Feather

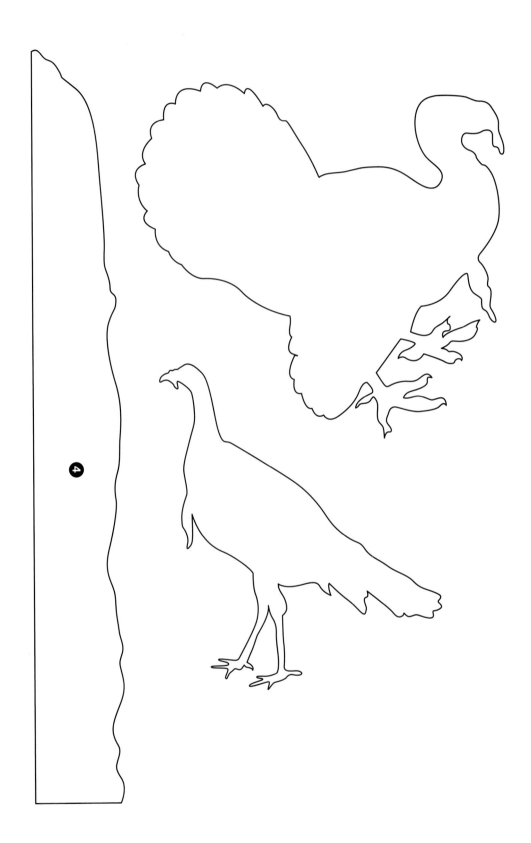

Rows in the Forest

Pillows

Pillows

Resources

Most of the items listed here are available from your local quilt shop. Web sites were correct at the time of publication.

Moose Country Quilts
www.moosecountryquilts.com
My Web site, including my current pattern line

Fabric and Batting

Fabrics by these and other manufacturers or designers: Benartex Fabrics, Hoffman Fabrics, Moda Fabrics, Alexander Henry Fabrics, and fabrics designed by Nancy Crow

Hobbs Bonded Fibers
200 S Commerce Dr
Waco, TX 76710
(800) 433-3357
www.hobbsbondedfibers.com
Heirloom Cotton Blend (80/20) batting

The Warm Company
954 E Union St
Seattle, WA 98122
(800) 234-WARM
www.warmcompany.com
Warm & Natural batting, Steam-A-Seam

Tools and Supplies

Add-A-Quarter Ruler by CM Designs
Available through your local notions supplier

Bernina of America, Inc.
3702 Prairie Lake Ct
Aurora, IL 60504
(630) 978-2500
www.berninausa.com
Sewing machines

Little Foot, Ltd.
(800) 597-7075
www.littlefoot.net
That Purple Thang by Lynn Graves

Martingale & Company
That Patchwork Place
20205 144th Ave NE
Woodinville, WA 98072-8478
(800) 426-3126
www2.martingale-pub.com
Bias Square Ruler

Olfa - North America
1536 Beech St
Terre Haute, IN 47804
(800) 962-OLFA
www.olfa.com
Rotary cutters and mats

Prym-Dritz USA
P.O. Box 5028
Spartanburg, SC 29304
www.dritz.com
Omnigrid rulers of all sizes